SECOND EDITION

2

STEP FORWARD

STANDARDS-BASED LANGUAGE LEARNING
FOR WORK AND ACADEMIC READINESS

SERIES DIRECTOR
Jayme Adelson-Goldstein

Ingrid Wisniewska

OXFORD
UNIVERSITY PRESS

TABLE OF CONTENTS

Unit	LESSON Key Objectives	LANGUAGE Vocabulary	Grammar
PRE-UNIT **The First Step** page 2 **Themes** ■ The alphabet, numbers, and the calendar ■ Personal information	■ Respond to personal information questions ■ Identify days and months	**Topic-Specific** ■ Classroom words; Greetings ■ Personal information ■ Days and dates **OPD Connection** ■ Meeting and Greeting ■ Personal Information ■ Numbers; The Calendar	■ The verb *be*
1 Learning to Learn page 4 **Themes** ■ Learning styles and tools ■ Workplace introductions	■ Identify personal learning styles ■ Identify effective study strategies ■ Use the simple present to describe study habits ■ Introduce self and others ■ Request clarification ■ Identify education and training options	**Topic-Specific** ■ Ways to learn English ■ Learning tools **OPD Connection** ■ Meeting and Greeting ■ Personal Information ■ A Classroom ■ Studying **Academic language** *transfer, transition*	■ The simple present with *want to*, *like to*, and *need to* ■ Information questions with simple present ■ *Yes/no* questions with simple present ■ Statements with *this*, *that*, *these*, and *those*
2 Getting Together page 18 **Themes** ■ Feelings and weather ■ Interrupting politely	■ Interpret information about feelings and weather ■ Identify and describe seasonal events ■ Use the future with *will* and *won't* to describe future plans ■ Ask for, give, and clarify directions ■ Interpret information about small talk ■ Interpret an invitation	**Topic-Specific** ■ Feelings ■ Weather ■ Reading temperatures **OPD Connection** ■ The Calendar ■ Feelings; Weather ■ Downtown; City Streets ■ Directions and Maps **Academic language** *energetic, relax*	■ Prepositions of time ■ The future with *will* ■ Information questions with *will* ■ *Yes/no* questions with *will* ■ Prepositions of location ■ Time expressions
3 Moving Out page 32 **Themes** ■ Household problems and repairs ■ Asking about regulations	■ Identify household problems and repairpeople ■ Recognize household maintenance ■ Identify housing features ■ Interpret classified ads ■ Compare different types of housing ■ Respond to housing ads ■ Evaluate ways to find housing ■ Interpret rental agreements	**Topic-Specific** ■ Household problems ■ Housing advertisements **OPD Connection** ■ The Home; Finding a Home ■ Apartments ■ Different Places to Live ■ Household Problems and Repairs **Academic language** *available, regulations*	■ The comparative ■ Questions and answers with *which* ■ Adverbs of degree with comparatives ■ *Yes/no* questions with *be + allowed*

Step Forward supports learners as they work to meet the *English Language Proficiency Standards for Adult Education* (ELPS) and the *College and Career Readiness Standards for Adult Education* (CCRS). See *Step Forward's* **Teacher Resource Center** for step-by-step lesson plans that list the level-specific ELP and CCR standards, and for other detailed correlations.

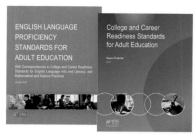

LANGUAGE STRATEGIES		COLLEGE & CAREER READINESS	
Reading & Writing	**Listening & Speaking**	**Critical Thinking**	**Collaboration**
■ Read the letters of the alphabet ■ Write contractions of the verb *be* ■ Read information on an ID card ■ Read and write the days and months	**Conversation** ■ Practice introductions **Focused Listening** ■ Listen for days and dates	**Critical thinking** ■ Recognize an address and telephone number ■ Sequence days and months ■ Recognize and associate ordinal numbers with dates	■ Speak so others can understand ■ Listen actively ■ Communicate information ■ Communicate verbally
■ Read about learning a new language ■ Write about learning styles ■ Read about adult education programs; interpret a course listing **Writing strategy** ■ Indent paragraphs **Reading strategy** ■ Use subheads to predict meaning	**Conversation** ■ Request clarification ■ Talk about education and job training **Focused Listening** ■ Listen to a conversation about studying for an exam ■ Listen to introductions **Pronunciation** ■ Check understanding using falling and rising intonation	**Critical thinking** ■ Reflect on personal learning styles ■ Compare study habits and personal learning styles ■ Setting goals **Problem solving** ■ Schedule study time into a busy work schedule	■ Understand teamwork ■ Work with others ■ Communicate verbally ■ Listen actively
■ Read and write about a favorite season ■ Read about future events ■ Write sentences about future events ■ Read about small talk ■ Read a party invitation **Writing strategy** ■ Use a topic sentence **Reading strategy** ■ Use examples to illustrate ideas	**Conversation** ■ Talk about how weather affects feelings ■ Discuss times and dates of future events ■ Give, get, and clarify directions **Focused Listening** ■ Listen for events and times on a calendar ■ Listen for directions **Pronunciation** ■ Use word stress for emphasis	**Critical thinking** ■ Reflect on a favorite season ■ Analyze scheduled events ■ Choose the dates and times of events ■ Examine routes on a map **Problem solving** ■ Resolve conflicts between scheduled events and childcare	■ Understand teamwork ■ Communicate information ■ Work with others ■ Communicate verbally
■ Read about a current home and a dream home ■ Write about your dream home ■ Read about ways to find an apartment ■ Read a rental agreement **Writing strategy** ■ Introduce the last point in a list with *finally* **Reading strategy** ■ Identify the purpose of a text	**Conversation** ■ Talk about household repairs ■ Ask about regulations in apartments and at work **Focused Listening** ■ Listen for features in a home ■ Listen for information about apartments **Pronunciation** ■ Practice falling and rising intonation with questions	**Critical thinking** ■ Compare and contrast homes ■ Interpret housing ads ■ Draw conclusions about types of housing ■ Summarize housing information ■ Interpret a rental agreement **Problem solving** ■ Determine whether to rent or buy a new home	■ Understand teamwork ■ Communicate information ■ Work with others ■ Communicate verbally

Unit	LESSON Key Objectives	LANGUAGE Vocabulary	Grammar
4 Looking for Work page 46 **Themes** ■ Jobs and job applications ■ Talking about job skills	■ Identify common jobs ■ Identify job application vocabulary ■ Evaluate job interview performance ■ Interpret job ads ■ Use the simple past to describe past events related to work and study ■ Respond to interview questions ■ Identify job training opportunities	**Topic-Specific** ■ Job applications ■ Jobs ■ Job interviews **OPD Connection** ■ The Workplace ■ Jobs and Occupations ■ Job Skills ■ Career Planning ■ Job Search ■ Interview Skills ■ Schools and Subjects **Academic language** *assistant, evaluate*	■ The simple past of regular verbs ■ Information questions with regular verbs in the simple past ■ Adverbs of manner
5 On the Job page 60 **Themes** ■ Pay stubs and the workplace ■ Requesting a schedule change	■ Identify parts of a pay stub ■ Identify workplace equipment ■ Identify appropriate workplace and school behavior ■ Use *might* to describe possibilities at work and in everyday life ■ Clarify directions on the job ■ Request a schedule change ■ Identify factors affecting job retention and advancement	**Topic-Specific** ■ Pay stub terms ■ Workplace equipment **OPD Connection** ■ Prepositions ■ The Workplace ■ Job Skills ■ Office Skills ■ Job Search ■ Job Safety ■ Office Work **Academic language** *attitude, cooperate, equipment, evaluation, promotion, regulations*	■ *Might* and *might not* ■ *Should* and *should not* ■ Making requests with *can* and *could*
6 On the Phone page 74 **Themes** ■ Phone bills and using phones ■ Apologizing and making excuses	■ Identify a phone bill ■ Identify different uses for phones ■ Identify reasons for being absent from work or school ■ Write an absence note ■ Use the present continuous and simple present ■ Take, interpret, and leave phone messages ■ Identify community services ■ Interpret data about volunteering	**Topic-Specific** ■ Phone bill terms ■ Phones and phone calls **OPD Connection** ■ The Telephone ■ Office Skills ■ A Bad Day at Work ■ Internet Research **Academic language** *contribute, volunteer*	■ The present continuous ■ Contrasting the present continuous and the simple present ■ Information questions with the simple present and present continuous ■ *Yes/no* questions with the simple present and present continuous ■ Verbs with direct and indirect objects

LANGUAGE STRATEGIES		COLLEGE & CAREER READINESS	
Reading & Writing	**Listening & Speaking**	**Critical Thinking**	**Collaboration**
- Read and write about a job interview - Read a job ad - Read about working and studying part-time - Write about past events - Read about changing careers - Read a job training chart **Writing strategy** - Sequence with time words **Reading strategy** - Navigate a web page	**Conversation** - Talk about jobs, education, and work experience - Talk about jobs and required skills - Ask and respond to interview questions - Talk about education and job training **Focused Listening** - Listen for information about job ads - Listen for job skills **Pronunciation** - Practice pronouncing syllables in present and past verbs	**Critical thinking** - Reflect on and draw conclusions about jobs - Analyze job interview behavior - Speculate about required job skills and education for jobs - Determine lengths of education and on-the-job training **Problem solving** - Determine opportunities for career development	- Understand teamwork - Communicate information - Work with others - Communicate verbally
- Read a pay stub - Read about workplace rules - Write about rules at work or school - Read about job performance skills and attitudes - Read a performance evaluation **Writing strategy** - Use informal greetings **Reading strategy** - Identify reasons	**Conversation** - Talk about workplace equipment - Talk about classroom and workplace regulations - Clarify job instructions - Request a schedule change - Talk about performance evaluations **Focused Listening** - Listen for appropriate work behavior - Listen for job instructions **Pronunciation** - Use intonation and word stress to interpret emotions	**Critical thinking** - Interpret figures on a pay stub - Compare and contrast appropriate workplace and school behavior - Analyze job performance skills **Problem solving** - Find solutions to difficulties at a new job	- Understand teamwork - Communicate information - Work with others - Communicate verbally
- Read a phone bill - Read about calling in sick - Write an absence note - Read and write phone messages - Read about community services - Read a bar chart about volunteering **Writing strategy** - Use formal greetings **Reading strategy** - Interpret links in web pages	**Conversation** - Talk about phones and phone usage - Talk about calling in sick - Leave and take phone messages - Apologize and make excuses - Talk about volunteering **Focused Listening** - Listen for information in phone messages - Listen for people's activities in the present **Pronunciation** - Practice the vowel sounds in *live* and *leave*	**Critical thinking** - Interpret information on a phone bill - Interpret a bar chart **Problem solving** - Resolve childcare problems due to illness	- Understand teamwork - Communicate information - Cooperate with others - Communicate verbally

| Unit | LESSON | LANGUAGE | |
	Key Objectives	Vocabulary	Grammar
7 What's for Dinner? page 88 **Themes** ■ Food containers and measurements ■ Offering and asking for help	■ Identify product containers ■ Interpret weights and measurements ■ Identify and compare product price information ■ Use count and noncount nouns to describe quantities of food ■ Ask for and give the location of merchandise ■ Interpret nutritional information ■ Interpret food labels	**Topic-Specific** ■ Container words ■ Weights, measurements, and equivalents **OPD Connection** ■ Back from the Market ■ A Grocery Store ■ Containers and Packaging ■ Weights and Measurements **Academic language** *conversion, equivalent*	■ Count and noncount nouns ■ Questions with *How many* and *How much* ■ Quantity words with noncount nouns ■ Review *There is/are*
8 Stay Safe and Well page 102 **Themes** ■ Illnesses and symptoms ■ Clarifying instructions	■ Identify and recommend medications ■ Describe symptoms of illnesses ■ Identify dental health services ■ Make medical appointments ■ Use the simple past of irregular verbs to describe accidents and injuries ■ Interpret prescription labels ■ Clarify instructions ■ Interpret simple first-aid procedures ■ Interpret a chart about accidents and injuries	**Topic-Specific** ■ Medications ■ Illnesses and symptoms **OPD Connection** ■ Symptoms and Injuries ■ Illnesses and Medical Conditions ■ A Pharmacy ■ First Aid **Academic language** *injured, instructions, medical*	■ The simple past of irregular verbs ■ *Yes/no* questions with the simple past of irregular verbs ■ *Wh-* questions with the simple past of irregular verbs ■ Review *have to* and *has to*
9 Money Matters page 116 **Themes** ■ Banking and ATMs ■ Responding to requests	■ Interpret personal finances ■ ATM instructions ■ Estimate personal budgets ■ Identify ways to save money ■ Use *because* and infinitives of purpose to give reasons and purpose ■ Use referents ■ Make returns or exchanges when shopping ■ Identify credit card safety procedures ■ Interpret a pie chart	**Topic-Specific** ■ Bank words ■ Using an ATM **OPD Connection** ■ Shopping ■ The Bank **Academic language** *feature, percent, purchase*	■ Purpose and reasons with *to* and *because* ■ Adjectives with *too* and *not... enough* ■ *Would like* with nouns and verbs

LANGUAGE STRATEGIES		COLLEGE & CAREER READINESS	
Reading & Writing	**Listening & Speaking**	**Critical Thinking**	**Collaboration**
■ Read about comparison shopping ■ Write about saving money ■ Read a recipe card ■ Write a recipe ■ Read about food and health ■ Read nutrition labels **Writing strategy** ■ Use a topic sentence **Reading strategy** ■ Apply information from reading to real-life problems	**Conversation** ■ Talk about containers, weights, and measurements ■ Talk about saving money at the supermarket ■ Talk about quantities ■ Offer and ask for help **Focused Listening** ■ Listen for ways to save money at the supermarket ■ Listen for quantities ■ Listen for the location of supermarket items **Pronunciation** ■ Practice pronouncing syllables in singular and plural nouns	**Critical thinking** ■ Interpret product price information ■ Compare and contrast weights and measurements ■ Examine the relationship between food and good health ■ Analyze values on nutrition labels **Problem solving** ■ Find solutions to an unhealthy diet	■ Work with others ■ Understand teamwork ■ Communicate verbally ■ Use math to solve problems and communicate
■ Read a review of dental health providers ■ Write about a medical visit ■ Read a prescription label ■ Read about preparing a first-aid kit ■ Read a pie chart about workplace injuries **Writing strategy** ■ Summarize a review **Reading strategy** ■ Use the parts of a web page	**Conversation** ■ Talk about illnesses and symptoms ■ Talk about accidents and injuries ■ Talk about workplace accidents ■ Talk to a pharmacist about prescription information ■ Clarify instructions **Focused Listening** ■ Listen for health problems and medications ■ Listen for the parts of a prescription label **Pronunciation** ■ Practice formal and relaxed pronunciation of *have to* and *has to*	**Critical thinking** ■ Speculate about the causes of accidents ■ Analyze prescription label instructions ■ Interpret a pie chart about workplace injuries **Problem solving** ■ Respond to workplace injuries	■ Listen actively ■ Communicate information ■ Work with others ■ Communicate verbally
■ Read bank statements, personal checks, and bills ■ Read and write about shopping for a major purchase ■ Write reasons for buying things ■ Read receipts and return forms ■ Read about protecting credit cards **Writing strategy** ■ Use sequence words **Reading strategy** ■ Identify points on a bulleted list	**Conversation** ■ Talk about ATMs and payment preferences ■ Talk about shopping for a major purchase ■ Talk about reasons for buying things ■ Talk about returning and exchanging items ■ Respond to customer requests **Focused Listening** ■ Listen for items in a budget ■ Listen for information to complete a return form **Pronunciation** ■ Practice *I like* and *I'd like*	**Critical thinking** ■ Analyze figures on bank statements ■ Sequence steps when using an ATM ■ Examine reasons for buying something ■ Analyze sales receipts and reasons for returns and exchanges ■ Analyze a pie chart about credit card fraud ■ Decide on a budget **Problem solving** ■ Analyze spending and manage credit card bills	■ Understand teamwork ■ Communicate information ■ Work with others ■ Communicate verbally

	LESSON		LANGUAGE	
Unit	**Key Objectives**	**Vocabulary**	**Grammar**	
10 Steps to Citizenship page 130 **Themes** ■ Citizenship and government ■ Making polite commands	■ Identify citizenship requirements ■ Identify government leaders ■ Identify community problems and solutions ■ Use *must* for obligation to describe community and transportation rules ■ Respond to police and security personnel requests and commands ■ Interpret information about the U.S. government	**Topic-Specific** ■ Citizenship words ■ Government officials **OPD Connection** ■ Government and Military Service ■ Civic Engagement ■ Traffic Signs **Academic language** *administrative, benefit, community, document, federal, role*	■ *Must* and *must not* ■ *Must* with adverbs of frequency ■ Comparing *must* and *should*	
11 Deal with Difficulties page 144 **Themes** ■ Emergencies and disasters ■ Making an emergency call	■ Identify crimes, emergencies, and natural disasters ■ Identify emergency services ■ Describe and report emergencies ■ Use the past continuous to describe emergencies ■ Identify and describe emergencies ■ Make emergency calls ■ Identify safety procedures for emergencies	**Topic-Specific** ■ Crimes and emergencies ■ Natural disasters **OPD Connection** ■ The Telephone ■ Crime ■ Emergencies and Natural Disasters ■ Emergency Procedures **Academic language** *injury, medical, occur*	■ The past continuous ■ Compare the past continuous and the simple past ■ Information questions in the past ■ *Yes/no* questions in the past ■ *There was/were*	
12 Take the Day Off page 158 **Themes** ■ Recreation and entertainment ■ Asking for opinions	■ Identify recreational facilities, activities, and entertainment genres ■ Describe weekend plans ■ Use the superlative to describe popular entertainment ■ Ask for and give opinions ■ Agree and disagree with others' opinions ■ Identify U.S. points of interest ■ Use maps for travel needs	**Topic-Specific** ■ Recreational activities ■ Months ■ Entertainment **OPD Connection** ■ Geography and Habitats ■ Places to Go ■ Outdoor Recreation ■ Winter and Water Sports ■ Individual Sports ■ Team Sports ■ Entertainment **Academic language** *relaxing*	■ The superlative ■ Using the comparative and the superlative ■ Agreeing and disagreeing	

LANGUAGE STRATEGIES		COLLEGE & CAREER READINESS	
Reading & Writing	**Listening & Speaking**	**Critical Thinking**	**Collaboration**
■ Read about community participation ■ Write about helping a community problem ■ Read about traffic rules ■ Write community rules ■ Read about the branches of the U.S. government and term limits **Writing strategy** ■ Separate a story into paragraphs **Reading strategy** ■ Combine information from different sources	**Conversation** ■ Discuss questions about government officials ■ Talk about community participation ■ Ask and answer questions about ID problems ■ Respond politely to officials ■ Make polite commands **Focused Listening** ■ Listen for office regulations ■ Listen for ID problems **Pronunciation** ■ Interpret polite and upset intonation	**Critical thinking** ■ Differentiate between federal, state, and local officials ■ Reflect on ways to resolve community problems ■ Analyze and calculate term limits for government officials **Problem solving** ■ Determine how to handle traffic violations	■ Listen actively ■ Communicate information ■ Work with others ■ Use math to solve problems and communicate
■ Read about a fire at home ■ Write about an emergency ■ Read about a flood ■ Read about emergency safety procedures ■ Read an emergency kit checklist ■ Write emergency safety procedures **Writing strategy** ■ Add details for vivid description **Reading strategy** ■ Read headings to determine if a text is useful	**Conversation** ■ Talk about natural disasters and emergencies ■ Practice making an emergency call ■ Ask for help ■ Make an emergency call in a workplace **Focused Listening** ■ Listen for information about accidents and emergencies ■ Listen for when to call 911 **Pronunciation** ■ Practice stressed syllables	**Critical thinking** ■ Interpret dates and facts about natural disasters ■ Differentiate between emergencies and non-emergencies ■ Draw conclusions about emergency kit items ■ Choose appropriate action during an emergency **Problem solving** ■ Respond appropriately to a hurricane warning	■ Understand teamwork ■ Communicate information ■ Work with others ■ Communicate verbally
■ Read about weekend activities ■ Write about weekend plans ■ Write opinions about sports ■ Read about places to visit in the U.S. ■ Read a map of the U.S. **Writing strategy** ■ Include supporting details **Reading strategy** ■ Identify location words	**Conversation** ■ Talk about recreational activities ■ Talk about weekend plans ■ Discuss fitness and free-time activities ■ Ask for and give opinions ■ Agree and disagree with opinions **Focused Listening** ■ Listen for weekend activity plans ■ Listen for descriptions of fitness activities ■ Listen for opinions about entertainment **Pronunciation** ■ Practice emphatic stress	**Critical thinking** ■ Speculate about weekend activities ■ Negotiate times and dates of recreational activities ■ Interpret facts about U.S. sights ■ Design a journey using a map of the U.S. **Problem solving** ■ Find solutions to reduce time spent watching TV	■ Understand teamwork ■ Communicate information ■ Work with others ■ Communicate verbally

"What's new?" is a question that often greets the arrival of a second edition, but let's start with the similarities between *Step Forward Second Edition* and its predecessor. This edition retains the original's effective instructional practices for teaching adult English language learners, such as focusing on learner outcomes, learner-centered lessons, thematic four-skill integration with associated vocabulary, direct instruction of grammar and pronunciation, focused listening, and sourced texts. It also preserves the instructional flexibility that allows it to be used in classes that meet twice a week, and those that meet every day. Perhaps most significantly, this edition continues to provide the differentiation support for teachers in multilevel settings.

The *College and Career Readiness Standards for Adult Education* (Pimentel, 2013) and the 2016 *English Language Proficiency Standards* echo the research by ACT, Parrish and Johnson, Wrigley, and others linking critical thinking skills, academic language, and language strategies to learners' academic success and employability. Rigorous language instruction is key to accelerating our learners' transition into family-sustaining jobs, civic engagement, and/or post-secondary education. *Step Forward Second Edition* has integrated civic, college, and career readiness skills in every lesson. Each *Step Forward* author considered adult learners' time constraints while crafting lessons that flow from objective to outcome, encouraging and challenging learners with relevant tasks that ensure their growth.

STEP FORWARD KEY CONCEPTS

Our learners' varied proficiency levels, educational backgrounds, goals, and interests make the English language classroom a remarkable place. They also create some instructional challenges. To ensure that your learners leave class having made progress toward their language and life goals, these key concepts underpin the *Step Forward* curriculum.

Effective instruction…

▶ acknowledges and makes use of learners' prior knowledge and critical thinking skills.

▶ helps learners develop the language that allows them to demonstrate their 21st century skills.

▶ contextualizes lessons to support learners' workplace, career, and civic goals.

▶ ensures that each lesson's learning objectives, instructions, and tasks are clear.

▶ differentiates instruction in order to accommodate learners at varying proficiency levels within the same class.

▶ provides informational text (including graphs, charts, and images) that builds and expands learners' knowledge.

STEP FORWARD COMPONENTS

Each level of *Step Forward* correlates to *The Oxford Picture Dictionary*. Each *Step Forward* level includes the following components:

Step Forward Student Book
Twelve thematic units focusing on everyday adult topics, each with six lessons integrating communication, workplace, and academic skills, along with language strategies for accuracy and fluency.

Step Forward Audio Program
The recorded vocabulary, focused listening, conversations, pronunciation, and reading materials from the *Step Forward* Student Book.

Step Forward Workbook
Practice exercises for independent work in the classroom or as homework, as well as "Do the Math" sections.

Step Forward Teacher Resource Center
An online collection of downloadable resources that support the *Step Forward* program. The *Step Forward* Teacher Resource Center contains the following components:

• *Step Forward* Lesson Plans: an instructional planning resource with detailed, step-by-step lesson plans featuring multilevel teaching strategies and teaching tips

• *Step Forward* Multilevel Activities: over 100 communicative practice activities and 72 picture cards; lesson materials that work equally well in single-level or multilevel settings

• *Step Forward* Multilevel Grammar Exercises: multilevel grammar practice for the structures presented in the *Step Forward* Student Book

• *Step Forward* Testing Program: tests for every unit in the *Step Forward* Student Book

• *Step Forward* Literacy Reproducible Activities: literacy activities that correspond to the *Step Forward Introductory Level* Student Book, intended to support pre-beginning or semi-literate level learners

• Correlations: correlations to national standards, including the *College and Career Readiness Standards* and the *English Language Proficiency Standards*

• *Step Forward* Answer Keys and Audio Scripts for the *Step Forward* Student Book and Workbook

Step Forward Classroom Presentation Tool
On-screen *Step Forward* Student Book pages, including audio at point of use and whole-class interactive activities, transform each Student Book into a media-rich classroom presentation tool in order to maximize-heads up learning. The intuitive, book-on-screen design helps teachers navigate easily from page to page.

I know I speak for the authors and the entire *Step Forward* publishing team when I say it's a privilege to serve you and your learners.

Jayme Adelson-Goldstein

Jayme Adelson-Goldstein, Series Director

WELCOME, LEARNERS!

Learning English is a challenge. *Step Forward* can help. Here are some ideas to try.

STUDY THE LISTS, CHARTS, AND NOTES
They give you information about English.

Vocabulary list

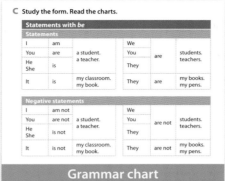

Grammar chart

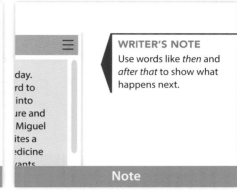

Note

BE BRAVE IN CLASS
Practice helps you use English.

ASK QUESTIONS
Questions help you understand.

COLLABORATE
Work with your classmates, and study alone, too.

Work with a partner

Work with a team

Work alone

The First Step

A LOOK AT
- The alphabet, numbers, and the calendar
- The verb *be*
- Personal information

1 Review the alphabet

1-02 **A Listen. Repeat the letters of the alphabet.**

A B C D E F G H I J K L M N O P Q R S T U V W X Y Z
a b c d e f g h i j k l m n o p q r s t u v w x y z

B Work with a partner. Choose a word in the box. Ask: How do you spell…?

chair	table	desk	pencil	board	homework

A: *How do you spell chair?*
B: *C-H-A-I-R*

2 Meet, greet, and say goodbye

1-03 **A Listen and read.**

Denise: Hello, Rick! How are you?

Rick: Fine, thank you!

Elena: Good morning!

Denise: Oh hi, Elena! Elena, this is Rick.

Rick: Hello, Elena. It's nice to meet you.

Elena: Nice to meet you, too.

Rick: Well, we're late for class. We have to go. Goodbye.

Elena: See you later!

B Work in groups of three. Practice the conversation. Use your own names.

3 The verb *be*

Complete the sentences with *am*, *is*, or *are*. Use contractions when possible.

1. I '_m___ fine.
2. You _____ happy.
3. We _____ in class.
4. Carla and Sam _____ married.
5. I _____ at school.
6. Elena _____ a new student.

4 Personal information

Look at the student ID card. Work with a partner. Ask and answer the questions.

1. What's her first name? __Mia__
2. What's her last name? _____
3. What's her address? _____
4. What's her phone number? _____
5. Where does she go to school? _____

Eastside Adult School

First name:	Last name:
Mia	Wong

Address:
1530 Hill St.
Los Angeles, CA 90001

Phone:
213-555-4768

5 Days and months

1-04

A Write the missing days and months. Then listen and check.

Days of the week:

Sunday ___Monday___ Tuesday _____ Thursday _____ Saturday

Months of the year:

January ___February___ March _____ May _____ July

_____ September _____ November _____

B Work with a partner. Follow the directions. Use the days and months in 5A.

1. Circle the day and month today.
2. Check (✓) the months with 30 days.

1-05

C Listen and read.

A: When is your birthday?
B: It's November 1st.
A: What day is that this year?
B: Thursday.

D Work with a partner. Practice the conversation. Use your own information.

Ordinal numbers	
1–first	11–eleventh
2–second	12–twelfth
3–third	13–thirteenth
4–fourth	14–fourteenth
5–fifth	15–fifteenth
6–sixth	16–sixteenth
7–seventh	17–seventeenth
8–eighth	18–eighteenth
9–ninth	19–nineteenth
10–tenth	20–twentieth

1 Learning to Learn

A LOOK AT
- Learning styles and tools
- Simple present with *want*, *like*, and *need*
- Workplace introductions

LESSON 1 VOCABULARY

1 Learn ways to study English

A Show what you know. Circle the words you know.

1. copy new words
2. practice with a partner
3. brainstorm ideas
4. use the computer
5. look up words
6. listen to recordings

1 Sam

2 Dana

3 Linda

4 Naomi

5 Fernando

6 Ahmed

B Listen and look at the pictures. What are these students doing? [1-06]

C Listen and repeat the words from 1A. [1-07]

D Write the vocabulary. Look at the pictures. Complete the sentences.

1. Naomi likes to ___use the computer___ .

2. Fernando likes to _____ in the dictionary.

3. Dana likes to _____ .

4. Linda and her friends like to _____ .

5. Ahmed likes to _____ .

6. Sam likes to _____ .

E Ask and answer this question with a partner: How do you like to study English?

4 Identify personal learning styles

2 Talk about learning tools

A Work with your classmates. Match the words with the picture.

_10_ tablet   _1_ flashcards   _12_ the Internet   _2_ pair

_9_ chart   _3_ group   _8_ marker   _5_ picture

_6_ dictionary   _1_ headphones   _4_ notebook   _7_ whiteboard

B Listen and check your answers. Take turns saying the words with a partner.

1-08

C Look at the picture. Mark the sentences *T* (true) or *F* (false).

__T__ 1. One student is using flashcards with her partner.

__F__ 2. A group is listening to recordings on a tablet.

__T__ 3. One student is looking up the word *goal* in the dictionary.

__T__ 4. One student is making a chart.

__F__ 5. Five students are writing in their notebooks.

__T__ 6. One pair of students is working on the Internet.

D Talk about it. Ask and answer the questions with your classmates.

1. How do you like to study English?
2. What other learning tools do you know?

NEED HELP?

I like to...
use the computer.
go on the Internet.
listen to recordings.
make a chart.

▶**TEST YOURSELF**

Copy the chart in your notebook. Write three ways to practice each skill.

Listening	Pronunciation	Vocabulary	Writing

1 Prepare to write

A Look at the pictures. What are they doing?

B Look at the pictures. Listen to the paragraph.
1-09

C Listen again and read the paragraph.
1-09

> Title ─────────── Learning a New Language
>
> by Dan Tanaka
>
>   I practice English every day. At home, I listen to conversations on my tablet. I repeat the new words. I also like to read stories. I underline the new words and look them up in the dictionary. Then I copy the words into my notebook and write an example sentence or a word with a similar meaning. In class, our teacher explains difficult words. I like to work in a group. I'm good at listening, but I don't speak a lot. It is easy to read English, but I want to speak more. I'm going to ask more questions in class.

WRITER'S NOTE
Remember to indent (leave a space) at the beginning of the first line of a paragraph.

D Check your understanding. Mark the sentences *T* (true) or *F* (false).

__T__ 1. Dan practices English every day.

__F__ 2. He doesn't like groups.

__F__ 3. He doesn't ask questions.

__F__ 4. He translates new words.

__F__ 5. He isn't a good listener.

__F__ 6. He speaks a lot.

E Listen to Dan and Mina talk about how they learn. Write *D* (Dan) or *M* (Mina).

1-10

_M_ listen to stories   _M_ use the Internet   _D_ write new words in a notebook

_D_ watch movies   _D_ read newspapers   _M_ play games

F Compare answers with your partner. Listen again and check your work.

1-10

2 Plan

A How do you like to learn English? Check (✓) the things that you do.

☐ 1. I go on the Internet   ☐ 4. I talk with classmates.

☐ 2. I watch movies.   ☐ 5. I make charts.

☐ 3. I read stories.   ☐ 6. I listen to recordings.

B Listen. Work with a partner. Practice the conversation. Use your own ideas.

1-11

A: How do you like to learn at home?

B: I like to watch movies. How about you?

A: I like to read stories.

C Get ready to write. Think about how you learn English. Answer the questions.

1. How do you practice English at home?

2. What do you listen to?

3. What do you read?

4. How do you practice English in class?

5. What is easy and what is difficult for you in English?

6. What do you want to improve?

3 Write

A Write a paragraph about how you learn English. Give your paragraph a title.

Learning English recordings

I _Read_ every day. At home, I listen to _audio_ . I read _books_ . In my English class, we _read aloud_ . I'm good at _reading_ , but I don't _studying_ a lot. It is easy for me to _read_ , but I want to _understand_ more. I want to improve my _speaking_ skills.

B Share your writing. Read your paragraph to a partner.

▸▸ TEST YOURSELF

Complete the following sentences. Share your responses with your teacher.

1. After this writing lesson, I can…

2. I need more help with…

1 Explore the simple present with *want to*, *like to*, and *need to*

A Listen and read the conversation. Mark the sentences *T* (true) or *F* (false).

1-12

Cam Tu: Hi, Brenda. I need to study math tonight. Do you want to study together?

Brenda: Yes, I do. I don't like to study alone.

Cam Tu: Well, I don't like to study after work, but I need to pass the test.

Brenda: I do too. Where do you want to study?

Cam Tu: Do you want to meet at the library tonight?

Brenda: Good idea!

___T___ 1. Cam Tu wants to study with Brenda.

___F___ 2. Brenda and Cam Tu need to study grammar.

B Analyze the sentences in the conversation. Underline the negative statements. What word makes a statement negative?

C Study the grammar. Read the charts.

The simple present with *want to*, *like to*, *need to*					
Affirmative statements					
I You We They	want like need	to study.	He She	wants likes needs	to study.

Negative statements						
I You We They	don't	want like need	to study.	He She	doesn't	want like need	to study.

D Work with the grammar. Circle the correct words.

1. Cam Tu (need / (needs)) to study math.

2. She (want / wants) to find a study partner.

3. Cam Tu and Brenda (want / wants) to work together.

4. Brenda (don't / doesn't) like to study alone.

5. Brenda and Cam Tu (don't / doesn't) want to study at home.

6. They (want / wants) to go to the library.

Play Audio *5/16/22*

2 Ask and answer information questions *p. 13 Lesson Plan*

A Study the grammar. Listen and repeat the conversations. *Using complete sentences.*

Information questions and answers	
A: What do you like to study? **B:** I like to study vocabulary.	**A:** When do you like to study? **B:** We like to study in the evening.
A: Where does she like to study? **B:** She likes to study in the kitchen.	**A:** How do they like to study? **B:** They like to study with flashcards.

B Check your understanding. Complete the questions and answers below.

1. **A:** <u>How does</u> Brenda like to study?
   B: She <u>likes to study</u> with a partner.
2. **A:** <u>what does</u> Brenda like to study?
   B: She <u>likes to study</u> grammar.
3. **A:** <u>Where do</u> you like to study?
   B: I <u>like to study</u> in my bedroom.
4. **A:** <u>When do</u> they like to study?
   B: They <u>like to study</u> in the evening.

C Match the questions with the answers.

<u>c</u>	1. What does she need to study?	a.	They want to meet at school.
<u>e</u>	2. When do they want to meet?	b.	They want to learn grammar.
<u>d</u>	3. How does he like to learn?	c.	She needs to study 10 new words.
<u>a</u>	4. Where do they want to meet?	d.	He likes to use flashcards.
<u>b</u>	5. What do they want to learn?	e.	They want to meet in the morning.

3 Ask and answer *yes/no* questions

A Study the grammar. Listen and repeat the conversations. *L5 P. 14*

Yes/no questions and answers		
A: Do you need to practice writing? **B:** Yes, I do. / No, I don't.	**A:** Does he like to read? **B:** Yes, he does. / No, he doesn't.	**A:** Do they want to study together? **B:** Yes, they do. / No, they don't.

B Check your understanding. Complete the questions and answers below.

A: <u>Do</u> you need to practice listening?
B: No, I <u>don't</u>. I need to practice writing.
A: <u>Do</u> you <u>want</u> to study together?
B: Yes, I <u>do</u>. Do you want to go to the library after class?

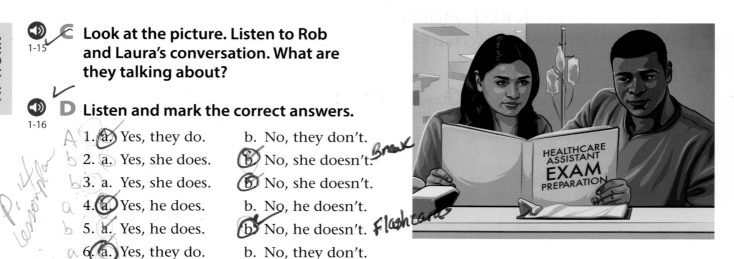

🔊 1-15 **C** Look at the picture. Listen to Rob and Laura's conversation. What are they talking about?

🔊 1-16 **D** Listen and mark the correct answers.

1. a. Yes, they do.   b. No, they don't.
2. a. Yes, she does.   b. No, she doesn't. *Break*
3. a. Yes, she does.   b. No, she doesn't.
4. a. Yes, he does.   b. No, he doesn't.
5. a. Yes, he does.   b. No, he doesn't. *Flashcards*
6. a. Yes, they do.   b. No, they don't.

🔊 1-16 **E** Listen again. Write two more *yes/no* questions about the conversation using *want*, *like*, or *need*. Tell the class.

4 Use *want*, *like*, and *need* to talk about your learning style

A Read the survey. Check (✓) your answers.

> **Learning Styles Survey**
>
> **1** How do you like to learn English?
> ☐ watch movies ☑ listen to songs ☐ write sentences ☐ talk with friends
>
> **2** How do you like to remember new words?
> ☑ look up words ☐ listen to recordings ☐ copy words ☑ use words in conversation
>
> **3** How do you like to study grammar?
> ☐ look at charts ☐ listen to examples ☑ read examples ☑ use grammar in conversation
>
> **4** How do you like to study English?
> ☐ on the Internet ☑ with recordings ☐ with books ☑ with classmates
>
> **5** What languages do you want to learn? I want to learn _Spanish_.
>
> **6** What learning tools do you need to use? I need to use _recordings_.

B Talk to a partner. Ask and answer questions from 4A. Use your own ideas.

A: *How do you like to learn English?*
B: *I like to practice English with my classmates. How do you like to remember new words?*

C Write four sentences about what your partner wants, likes, and needs.

She likes to listen to songs.

▶▶ TEST YOURSELF

Close your book. Use your notebook. Write five questions to ask someone about his or her study habits. Use *Where*, *How*, *What*, *When*, and *Do* and the simple present. Then write the answers to your questions.

PG 17 Lesson Plan

1 Listen to learn: introducing yourself and others

A Look at the pictures. What is happening in each one? *People Are Making Introductions*

1
Haruko
Kenji
Ling

2
Mr. Singh
Zoila
Ms. Morgan

3
Chanda
Barbara
Archir

1-17
B Listen to the conversations. Write the correct names in the blanks.

1-17
C Listen again. Match the people with the questions.

  b 1. Haruko   a. What's your name again?

  c 2. Ms. Morgan   b. Excuse me? What's your name?

  a 3. Barbara   c. How do you spell your first name?

2 Practice your pronunciation *p. 17*

1-18
A Listen to the falling and rising intonation. Then listen again and repeat.

1. What's your name? ↘   3. What's your name again? ↗

2. My name's Ling. L-I-N-G. ↘   4. Ling? L-I-N-G? ↗

1-19
B Read the conversation. Check (✓) *Falling* or *Rising*.
Then listen and check your answers.

	Falling	Rising
A: What's your name?	✓	
B: Anga.	✓	
A: Anga—is that A-N-G-A?		✓
B: That's right.	✓	

NEED HELP?

Falling and rising intonation

Statements and information questions usually use falling intonation.

Use rising intonation to check your understanding.

3 Practice statements with *this, that, these,* and *those*

A Listen and read the conversation. Who is Ned introducing?

Ned: Hi, everyone. This is my friend Emmy.

Rita: What's your name again?

Emmy: Emmy.

Rita: Is that E-M-M-Y?

Emmy: That's right.

Rita: Hi, Emmy. I'm Rita, and this is Alma.

Emmy: Nice to meet you.

B Study the grammar. Listen and repeat.

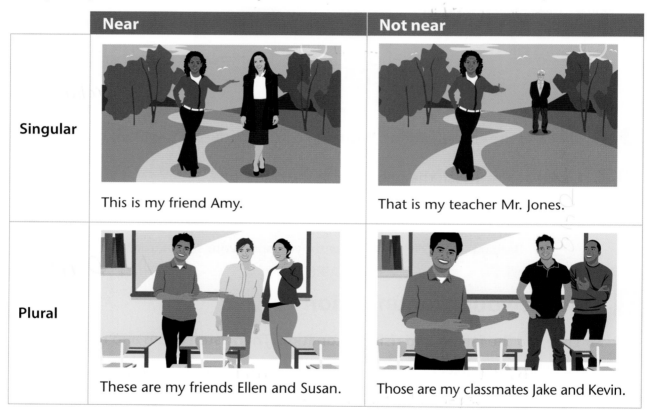

	Near	Not near
Singular	This is my friend Amy.	That is my teacher Mr. Jones.
Plural	These are my friends Ellen and Susan.	Those are my classmates Jake and Kevin.

C Talk to a partner. Describe people in your classroom. Use the examples in 3B.

4 Make conversation: clarifying

A Work with a partner. Make a new conversation.

A: Hi, _____ . _____ .
B: What's your name again? *Clarify*
C: _____ .
B: Is that _____ ?
C: Yes. That's right.
B: Hi, _____ . I'm _____ .
C: Nice to meet you.

B Present your conversation to another pair. Observe their conversation.

AT WORK ▸ Workplace introductions *Talk about P. 19*

A Listen to different ways to introduce someone. Which introduction is more formal?

1-22

formal (boss, new employees) *INFORMAL (co-workers, friends)*

A: Good morning! Allow me to introduce Mr. Roberts. He's visiting our office today.

B: Good morning, everyone.

A: Jody, this is Bob. Bob works with me in the clinic.

B: Hi, Bob. How are you?

B Think about it. Work with a partner. Ask and answer the questions.

1. Who are these people? Where are they?
2. What are the differences between these two types of introductions? Why are they different?

C Work in a group of three. Practice the introductions in A. Use your own names and continue the conversations.

▸▸ TEST YOURSELF

Act out this situation with a classmate. Take turns with each role.

Student A: Introduce your partner to five classmates.
Student B: Greet your classmates.

[handwritten: Diploma: receptionist, cust serv rep]
[handwritten: Certificate: plumber, mechanic]
[handwritten: Degree: engineer, doctor]

1 Build reading strategies *[handwritten: P. 21]*

A Read the definitions. Then brainstorm jobs that require a diploma, certificate, or degree.

When you study at...	for...	you can get...
an adult high school	3 months to 1 year	a GED or high school diploma
a community college or technical college	2 years	an associate's degree (AA or AS)
a college or university	4–5 years	a bachelor's degree (BA or BS)
a technical school or vocational school	1 month–1 year	a technical or vocational certificate

ACADEMIC

B Look at the subheadings on the web page. What types of classes *[handwritten: P. 21]* do you think are in each category?

C Read the information about adult education programs. *[handwritten: 5/16]* Which classes are work-related?

[handwritten: P. 21]

Adult Education Program

Our adult education program helps students make the transition[1] into academic study or a new career[2]. Our friendly staff can help you choose a class that is right for you. Let us help you follow your dreams and achieve your goals!

BASIC SKILLS

Do you need to prepare for the High School Equivalency Exam? These online classes will help you improve your English language skills and also your reading, writing, and math skills.

[handwritten: help language, reading writing Math]

ADULT TRANSITIONS

Are you just starting college or returning to college after a break? Do you want to apply for an AA or BA college degree program? These classes will help you improve your academic study skills and teach you how to choose college classes and get financial aid.

[handwritten: help choose college classes]

VOCATIONAL STUDIES

Do you want to start a career, change your job, or get a better salary? These classes help workers in a variety of jobs to develop their skills.

[handwritten: help change jobs]

Download our full course catalog here, or contact our program coordinator about other credit and non-credit classes, and to learn how to transfer[3] credits to other programs.

[handwritten: How do you get a catalog?]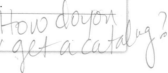

[1] transition: change from one situation or state to a new one
[2] career: a job that needs special training and develops over a period of time
[3] transfer: to move something from one place to another place

> **READER'S NOTE**
> Use subheadings to predict what the text is about.

 D Listen and read the article again. Which classes do you want to learn more about?
1-23

E Mark the sentences *T* (true) or *F* (false).

_F_ 1. These courses are for children and adults.

_F_ 2. The Basic Skills classes give you job training.

_T_ 3. You need a computer for the GED class.

_F_ 4. The Adult Transitions classes give you a college degree.

_T_ 5. The Vocational Studies classes can help you get a job.

F Complete the sentences. Use the words in the box.

| career | certificate | transition | transfer | vocational |

1. A GED _Certificate_ is the same as a high school diploma.
2. You need to get _vocational_ training to be a mechanic.
3. Academic study skills can help you make the _transition_ to a degree program.
4. You can sometimes _transfer_ credits from one school to a different school.
5. It's important to get the right education for your chosen _career_.

2 Interpret a course listing

A Read the course listing. Take turns describing the courses.

Adult education courses this summer

Title	Dates	Days	Time	Location/Teacher	Cost
Office Technology	7/11/18 – 8/29/18	W, F	6–9 p.m.	B12/Mr. Gomez	$120
College Writing Skills	7/9/18 – 8/24/18	M, F	7–9 p.m.	C12/Ms. Stone	$90
Food Safety and Preparation	7/14/18 – 8/30/18	Sat	10–11 a.m.	D19/Ms.King	$100

A: The Office Technology class meets on Wednesdays and Fridays from 6:00 to 9:00.

B: The College Writing Skills class costs $90.

A: Ms. King teaches the Food Safety class.

B Match each class with one of the categories from the catalog page in 1C.

C Think about it. Talk about these questions with your classmates.

1. Who are these classes useful for? Which of them are you interested in?
2. What kind of classes or job training do you need?
3. What are your goals for your training and education? Make a list.

⏻ BRING IT TO LIFE

Do research on the Internet or in your community and look for two classes or programs that could help you reach your goals. Report back to your class about the courses.

TEAMWORK & LANGUAGE REVIEW

A Work with a team. Look at the picture. Ask and answer the questions.

1. Where are these people?
2. What are they doing?
3. What objects in the picture are also in your classroom?
4. What objects in this classroom do you often use to study?
5. What do you like about the classroom? Why?
6. What is the man in yellow saying? How do you know?
7. Which group or pair in the picture do you want to work with? Why?

B Work with a team. Put the conversation in the correct order. Then rewrite the conversation using your own ideas.

Three students meet at the campus library.

__1__ **Cathy:** Hi, Victor. I want to introduce my friend Elise.

_____ **Elise:** That's right.

_____ **Elise:** Elise.

_____ **Elise:** Yes, I do. How about you? Where do you study?

_____ **Elise:** Nice to meet you.

_____ **Victor:** Hi, Elise. I'm Victor.

_____ **Victor:** Is that E-L-I-S-E?

_____ **Victor:** What's your name again?

_____ **Victor:** Do you like to study in the library?

_____ **Victor:** I like to study on my tablet in the coffee shop.

C Role-play a situation in a new class. Introduce yourself and a friend to your group. Ask and answer questions about how you like to study. Then present your role-play to the class.

D Work with a team. Read the chart about Lisa's goals. Use *first*, *next*, *then*, and *after that* to talk about her goals.

Lisa's long-term goal is…

First, she wants to…

Next, she needs to…

> **Lisa's long-term goal: To get work as a childcare worker**
>
> *Lisa's plan*
> 1. Get First Aid and CPR training/certificate
> 2. Prepare a resume that lists childcare experience
> 3. Check websites and bulletin boards in the local community for jobs

E Do you have any other ideas to help Lisa? Brainstorm ideas and discuss them with your team.

F Talk to your classmates. What are your educational or work training goals? Make a list for your group.

G Plan your goals. Complete a chart in your notebook. Use the chart in D as a model.

H Interview classmates about their goals.

A: *Hi, Alexa. What is your long-term goal?*

B: *I want to work as a chef.*

A: *That's great! What do you need to do first?*

PROBLEM SOLVING

 A Listen and read about Noreen.
1-24

> Noreen works full time every day. She also has a part-time job on the weekend. She goes to school three nights a week. She likes her class and her teacher. But Noreen is usually very tired after work. She can't do her homework, and then she can't get good grades.

B Work with your classmates. Answer the questions.

1. What is Noreen's problem?
2. What can she do? Think of two or three solutions to her problem.

UNIT

2 Getting Together

A LOOK AT
- Feelings and weather
- The future with *will*
- Interrupting politely

LESSON 1 VOCABULARY

1 Learn words for feelings

A Show what you know. Circle the words you know.

1. bored   2. frustrated   3. sleepy   4. surprised   5. energetic   6. upset

Donna

Jai

Tim

Ellen and Rosa

Bob

Patricia

B Listen and look at the pictures. What are these people doing?
1-25

C Listen and repeat the words from 1A.
1-26

D Write the vocabulary. Look at the pictures. Complete the sentences.

1. On sunny days, Bob is _energetic_ and goes jogging in the park.
2. When Ellen and Rosa see the dark clouds, they are _____ .
3. Jai is driving slowly because of the snow, and his children are _____ .
4. It was very windy last night, and now there's a tree on Patricia's car. She's _____ .
5. It's raining, and Donna can't go out to play. She's _____ .
6. On hot days, Tim feels very _____ and can't study.

E Talk to a partner. Ask and answer questions about the people in 1B.

A: How does Donna feel?   A: Why?

B: She is bored.   B: Because it's raining, and she wants to play soccer.

2 Talk about the weather

A Work with your classmates. Match the words with the pictures. Use the thermometer to add the missing temperatures.

_____ / 27°C

4 32°F / _____

6 _____ / 10°C

8 84°F / _____

_____ cool

_____ foggy

_____ freezing

_____ warm

_____ humid

_____ icy

_____ lightning

_____ snowstorm

__1__ thunderstorm

B Listen and check your answers. Then practice the words with a partner.

1-27

C Look at the pictures in 2A. Complete the conversations.

1. **A:** Wow! It's raining a lot. This is a bad _thunderstorm_ !

   B: Yes, and did you see the _____ ? Let's go into the house!

2. **A:** Brr. It's 32 degrees. It's _____ . Be careful. The sidewalk is _____ .

   B: OK. I love a good _____ . The city looks so white and clean.

3. **A:** I'm so frustrated. I can't see anything. It's very _____ .

   B: And I need a sweater. It's _____ outside.

4. **A:** Ugh! It's 84 degrees. It's so _____ !

   B: I know. And there's 98% humidity. I hate _____ weather.

D Think about it. Ask and answer the questions with your classmates.

1. How does weather affect your mood?

2. How do you feel when it's _____ ?

NEED HELP?

There's...	It's...
a thunderstorm.	snowing.
a snowstorm.	humid.
lightning.	25 degrees.

▶▶**TEST YOURSELF**

Use your notebook. Copy the chart.
Write six words for feelings and six words
for the weather in the chart.

	Feelings	Weather
good		
bad		

1 Prepare to write

A Look at the picture. What are the people doing? How are they feeling?

B Look at the picture. Listen to the paragraph.

1-28

vendors

farmers' market

baked goods

fruit and vegetables

musicians

C Listen again and read the paragraph.

1-28

> **My Favorite Season**
> **by Ana Diaz**
>
> Summer is a wonderful season in Eugene, Oregon. The weather is usually warm and sunny, and it's rarely humid. I'm always energetic in summer. It's perfect weather for hiking or cycling. Because of the warm weather, there are many outdoor events, such as the music festival and the county fair. I also love summer because I sell fresh fruit and vegetables at the weekly farmers' market. It is every Wednesday from June to October. Before the market, we're busy picking fruit and vegetables on our farm. At the farmers' market there are musicians and different kinds of food like pizza, tacos, and hot dogs. After the market, I relax with a glass of lemonade or some ice cream—coffee ice cream is my favorite!

WRITER'S NOTE
Focus your paragraph on one main idea. Use a topic sentence to introduce the main idea.

D Check your understanding. Mark the sentences *T* (true) or *F* (false).

___F___ 1. In summer, Ana often feels bored.

_____ 2. Summer is cool in Eugene.

_____ 3. There is a music festival once a year.

_____ 4. There is a farmers' market once a month in summer.

_____ 5. Ana is a vendor at the market.

_____ 6. After the market, Ana relaxes with pizza.

◀)) E Listen and write the dates of the community events in the flyer.
1-29

Enjoy the seasons! Year-round fun for the whole family!

St. Patrick's
Day Parade
_____

Garden Show
_____

Country Music
Festival
_____

Seafood Festival
_____

Pumpkin Patch
_____

Snow and Ice Festival
_____

◀)) F Compare dates with your partner. Listen again and check your work.
1-29

2 Plan

A Think about your favorite season. Complete the chart.

Favorite season	Weather	Feelings	Events you like

◀)) B Listen. Then work with a partner. Ask and answer questions about your chart.
1-30

<table>
<tr><td colspan="2">NEED HELP?</td></tr>
<tr><td>There's a...
concert, festival, dance, fair,
show, picnic, party
on September 10th, in January</td></tr>
</table>

3 Write

A Write a paragraph about your favorite season. Use your notes from 2A.

My Favorite Season

_____ is my favorite season. The weather is _____ and _____ , but it isn't _____ .
I always feel _____ in the _____ . I love to _____ and _____ . There's a _____
_____ . I usually _____ with my friends. Before the _____ , we usually _____ .
After the _____ we often _____ .

B Share your paragraph. Read your paragraph to a partner.

▶▶ TEST YOURSELF

Complete the following sentences. Share your responses with your teacher.

1. After this writing lesson, I can…   2. I need more help with…

1 Focus on the future with *will*

A Listen and read the conversation between Lara and Ana. Answer the questions.

1. When will Lara visit Ana?

   _____

2. How will she travel?

   _____

B Analyze the sentences in the conversation. Which verbs tell us that they are talking about the future?

C Study the grammar. Read the charts.

The future with *will*						Contractions
Affirmative statements						will = 'll
I			We			I'll visit in August.
You	will	visit in August.	You	will	visit in August.	They'll visit in August.
He She It			They			

Negative statements						Contractions
I			We			will not = won't
You	will not	visit in July.	You	will not	visit in July.	You won't visit in July.
He She It			They			He won't visit in July.

D Work with the grammar. Complete the sentences about Lara's and Ana's plans in 1A.

1. Ana ___will___ have some free time in August.
2. Lara _____ visit Ana in August.
3. She _____ take the train.
4. Lara _____ buy her plane ticket today.
5. Ana and Lara _____ be happy to see each other again.

2 Explore asking and answering questions with *will*

🔊 1-32 **A** Study the grammar. Listen and repeat the conversations. When do we **not** use contractions?

Information questions and answers
A: When will they meet?   **B:** They'll meet in August.
A: How long will she stay with Ana?   **B:** She'll stay for one week.

Yes/no questions and short answers
A: Will Lara travel by train?   **B:** No, she won't.
A: Will they go to the music festival?   **B:** Yes, they will.

B Practice asking questions about a work schedule. Read Peter's yearly planner. Complete the questions and answers.

Information questions and answers

1. **A:** <u>When will</u> Peter <u> go </u> to the sales meeting?

   B: <u>He'll go in January.</u>

2. **A:** _____ he _____ in February?

   B: _____

Yes/no questions and short answers

3. **A:** <u>Will</u> Peter _____ by train to San Francisco?

   B: _____

4. **A:** _____ Peter _____ a vacation in April?

   B: _____

January
Go to sales meeting in New York

February
Visit office in Mexico

March
Go by plane to San Francisco Office

April
Take a vacation

3 Practice: prepositions of time with *will*

A Complete the chart below. Use the words in the box.

| Monday | 3 p.m. | 2021 | December | Friday, January 22nd | 8:30 a.m. |
| ~~11 a.m.~~ | Thursday, August 3rd | 9:15 p.m. | April 2019 | Saturday |

at + time	*in* + month/year	*on* + day/date
11 *a.m.*		

B Work in pairs. Complete the information about yourself. Then ask and answer questions to find out your partner's information.

What are three things you will do before the end of this week?

Day _____ Time _____ Event _____

Day _____ Time _____ Event _____

Day _____ Time _____ Event _____

What are three things you will do before the end of this year?

Month _____ Date _____ Event _____

Month _____ Date _____ Event _____

Month _____ Date _____ Event _____

A: *What will you do before the end of this week?*

B: *I'll have dinner with my family on Saturday at 6:00. What will you do before the end of this year?*

A: *I'll start a new job on December 2nd.*

NEED HELP?

Time expressions

Right now it is Friday, August 5, 2017, at 3:30 p.m.

This time tomorrow = Saturday at 3:30 p.m.

On Wednesday = Wednesday of next week (August 10)

Three months from now = November 2017

Five years from now = August 2022

4 Practice talking about the future

A Read the chart. Write your answers.

Think about your future		
	at 11 a.m. tomorrow	on Wednesday
1. Where will you be?		
2. How will you feel?		
	three months from now	five years from now
3. Where will you live?		
4. What job will you have?		

B Interview a partner. Ask and answer the questions in 4A.

A: *Where will you be at 11 a.m. tomorrow?*

B: *I'll be at work.*

▶▶ **TEST YOURSELF**

Write six sentences about your future and your partner's future. Use the ideas in 3B and 4A.

At 11 a.m. tomorrow, I'll be at home. Samuel will be at school.

1 Listen to learn: give and get directions

A Look at the pictures. Match the directions with the pictures.

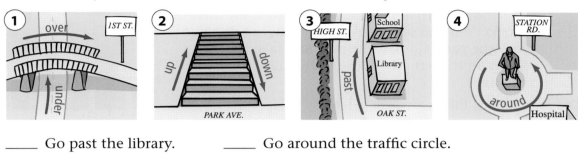

_____ Go past the library.   _____ Go around the traffic circle.

_____ Go up the steps.   _____ Go over the bridge.

B Listen and write the destinations in the chart below.
1-33

C Listen again. Write the directions.
1-33

	Destination	Directions
1.		
2.		
3.		
4.		

2 Practice your pronunciation

A Listen to the stressed words in these conversations.
1-34

1. **A:** Do I take the next street on the left?
   B: No, take the <u>second</u> street on the left.

2. **A:** Do I go over the bridge?
   B: No, go <u>under</u> the bridge.

3. **A:** Do I go up the steps?
   B: No, go <u>down</u> the steps.

4. **A:** Do I go past the bank?
   B: No, go past the <u>post office.</u>

B Listen again and repeat.
1-34

C Listen and complete the questions. Then underline the stressed words in the answers.
1-35

1. **A:** Do I take the _____ street on the _____ ?
   B: No, take the first street on the right.

2. **A:** Do I go _____ the _____ ?
   B: No, go past the supermarket.

3. **A:** Do I go _____ the _____ ?
   B: No, go over the bridge.

4. **A:** Do I go _____ the _____ ?
   B: No, go around the post office.

D Practice the conversations in 2C with a partner.

3 Practice using conjunctions *and* and *but*

A Read the directions. Underline the conjunctions *and* and *but*.

Diego: How do I get to your house from the train station?

Chul: Turn right when you come out of the train station. Go down the hill to the bridge, but don't go over the bridge. Turn left and follow the road for three blocks. You will see a park on the left, but don't go into the park. Go past the park and take the next street on the left. My house is the third house on the right.

Diego: Thanks! I'll see you there later.

B Think about the grammar. When do we use *but* instead of *and*?

C Study the grammar. Listen and repeat.

1-36

Conjunctions	
and	*but*
Go over the bridge. Turn right.	Go straight on 3rd Street. Don't go up the steps.
Go over the bridge **and** turn right.	Go straight on 3rd Street, **but** don't go up the steps.

D Talk to a partner. Read the map. Complete the directions.

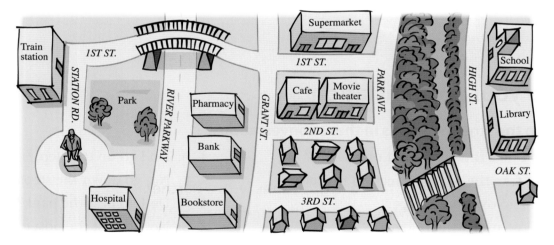

1. **From the hospital to the pharmacy:** Go straight on River Parkway, _____ don't go under the bridge. It's across from the _____ .

2. **From the library to the bookstore:** Go down the steps, _____ don't turn on Park Avenue. Go straight on 3rd Street. It's next to the _____ .

3. **From the movie theater to the library:** Turn right on Park Avenue _____ go up the stairs. It's on the corner of _____ and _____ .

4. **From the train station to the bank:** Go over the bridge _____ turn right on Grant Street. It's between the _____ and the _____ .

4 Make conversation: asking for and giving directions

A Work with a partner. Make a new conversation.

A: Excuse me. How do I get to _____ from _____ ?

B: Go _____ . Then _____ and _____ .

A: Go _____ and _____ ?

B: Yes, that's it. Then go _____ . The _____ is on the _____ .

A: Thank you very much.

B: No problem.

B Present your conversation to another pair. Observe their conversation.

AT WORK > ## Interrupting politely

1-37

A Practice your conversation skills. Listen to different ways to interrupt politely.

A: I'm sorry to interrupt you, but where will the sales meeting be?

B: Oh, that's OK. It'll be in the main conference room. Go past the elevator and turn right.

A: Excuse me. Where are the clean knives and forks?

B: They're in the supply closet. Just go around the corner.

B Talk to a partner. Practice the conversations in A.

C Think about it. Ask and answer the questions with a partner.

1. Who are these people? What is the relationship between them?

2. What are the differences between these two ways of interrupting someone? Why are they different?

3. What are some other situations when you need to interrupt someone?

> **NEED HELP?**
>
> Ways to interrupt
> Excuse me.
> Pardon me.
> Sorry to interrupt.
> Sorry to bother you.

▶▶ TEST YOURSELF

Act out this situation with a classmate. Take turns with each role. Use the community in this lesson or your own community.

Student A: Interrupt someone on the street. Ask for directions to the park.
Student B: Help someone who interrupts you. Give directions to the park.

1 Build reading strategies

A Read the sentences. Match them with the vocabulary.

1. I feel sad. I don't *feel like* going to a party tonight.

2. It's polite to *look directly at* someone when you say hello.

3. I like to talk to my friends, but it's difficult to talk to *people I don't know.*

____ strangers   ____ make eye contact   ____ be in the mood for

B Preview the title and the photo in the article below. What is the article about?

C Read the article. Where and why do people make small talk?

How to Make Small Talk

Small talk is a way to start a conversation. Sometimes, people make small talk with strangers, for example, at a bus stop or at a doctor's office. Students make small talk with their classmates before class starts. People also make small talk at parties.

For some people, small talk is very easy, but other people get nervous.[1] They don't know what to say. According to Kenneth Beare of *About.com*, sports, TV programs, and movies are good topics for small talk. The weather is also a good topic. People often begin a conversation with a statement about the weather. They say,

"It's a beautiful day," or "It's freezing today." Some people start a conversation with a compliment[2] about a piece of clothing or jewelry, for example, "That's a great color on you," or "I love your earrings."

Sometimes people don't want to talk. Before you begin a conversation, make eye contact with the person. Wait for the person to look at you and smile. The smile says, "It's OK. Let's talk." Small talk is a good way to meet people and make friends.

For more advice about how to make small talk, search online with the key words "small talk" and "tips".

[1]nervous: worried; a little upset
[2]compliment: say something nice about another person

READER'S NOTE

Writers use examples to illustrate their ideas. In paragraph 2, "I love your earrings," is an example of a compliment.

Source: *About.com*

1-38

D Listen and read the article again. Do you think small talk is easy or difficult?

E Read the questions. Fill in the bubble next to the correct answer.

1. What is the main topic of the article?
   (a) how to be confident
   (b) how to start a conversation
   (c) how to help people

2. The bus stop and the doctor's office are examples of places to _____ .
   (a) meet friends
   (b) talk to strangers
   (c) feel nervous

3. Sports and TV are examples of _____ .
   (a) conversation topics
   (b) popular topics
   (c) compliments

4. Look at paragraph 3. The author says: "Wait for the person to look at you and smile." What does a smile mean in this context?
   (a) Hello, how are you?
   (b) I'm feeling nervous.
   (c) I'm not in the mood to talk.

F Complete the sentences. Use the words in the box.

compliment	in the mood	nervous	strangers

1. People sometimes make small talk with _____ at the doctor's office.

2. Some people feel _____ about making small talk.

3. Sometimes people are not _____ for small talk.

4. One way to start a conversation is with a _____ .

2 Read an invitation

A Read the invitation. Answer the questions.

1. Who is the party for? <u>the technology department</u>

2. Who will bring the food? _____

3. When will the party start? _____

4. Where will the co-workers meet? _____

The Technology Department Annual Office Party

Bring your favorite food or drink.
Meet your co-workers! Have fun!

When: **Friday, September 23rd**
Time: **Noon-3 p.m.**
Place: **Second floor conference room**

B Think about it. Talk about the questions with your classmates.

1. Do you like parties with co-workers, family, or friends? Why or why not?

2. How do you feel about talking to people at parties?

3. How would you start a conversation with a co-worker at a social event?

⏻ BRING IT TO LIFE

Start a conversation in English with someone at school, at work, or in your neighborhood. Make small talk. Tell the class about your conversation.

A Work with a team. Look at the picture. Answer the questions.

1. Describe the people in the picture. What are they doing? How are they feeling?
2. Describe the weather.
3. What are the people selling or buying?
4. Why do people enjoy this kind of event?
5. What do you like about going to a farmers' market?

B Write a story about two people in the picture. The story is about their plans for next weekend.

Jim and Mario are musicians. They play music at the farmers' market. Next weekend...

C With your class, draw a map of the area near your school. Mark as many places as you can on the map, including a local farmers' market.

D Work with a team. Write a set of directions from the school to one place on the map your class made in C. Present your directions to the class. They will name your destination.

E Read the questionnaire. Copy the chart in your notebook.
Ask and answer the questions. Then take notes in your chart.

How do you feel...

- when you speak in front of the class?
- about starting conversations with strangers?
- when you go to a party?
- when someone gives you flowers?
- when you travel by plane?
- when there is a thunderstorm?

	you	Classmate 1	Classmate 2	Classmate 3
speak in class	confident			

F Use the information in your chart to write a summary
of your team's feelings in each situation.

*Our survey results show that three out of five of us feel nervous
when we speak in front of the class, but two of us feel calm.*

G Report your results to the class.

PROBLEM SOLVING AT HOME

1-39
A Listen and read about Gina.

There's an office party on Friday night. Gina isn't really in the mood for a party because she finds it difficult to make small talk with her co-workers. She also doesn't want to leave her children home alone at night. Gina's mother, Sofia, sometimes takes care of the children, but on Friday nights she likes to stay home and watch her favorite TV show.

B Work with your classmates. Answer the questions.

1. What is Gina's problem?
2. What can she do? Think of two or three solutions to her problem.

3 Moving Out

A LOOK AT
- Household problems and repairs
- The comparative
- Asking about regulations

LESSON 1 VOCABULARY

1 Learn about common household problems

A Show what you know. Circle the words you know.

1. dripping faucet
2. broken door
3. leaking pipe
4. mice
5. no electricity
6. cracked window

🔊 1-40 **B** Listen and look at the pictures. What's wrong in each room?

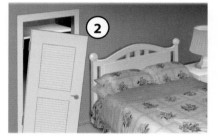

🔊 1-41 **C** Listen and repeat the words from 1A.

D Write the vocabulary. Look at the picture. Complete the sentences.

1. There's <u>no electricity</u> in the basement.
2. There's a _____ in the living room.
3. There's a _____ in the bathroom.
4. There's a _____ in the kitchen.
5. There's a _____ in the bedroom.
6. There are _____ in the garage.

E Ask your partner about the household problems in each room.

A: *What's wrong in the bathroom?*

B: *There's a dripping faucet.*

2 Talk about household repairs

A Work with your classmates. Match the words with the pictures.

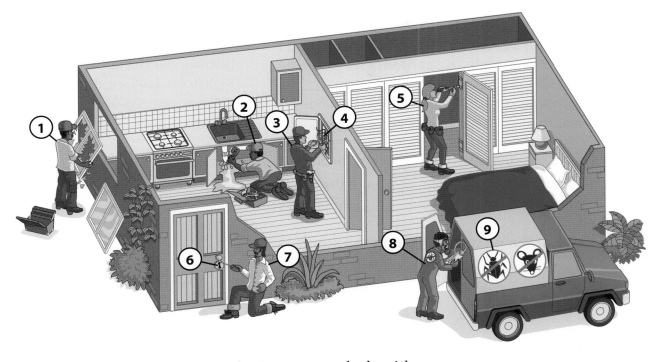

_____ carpenter   _____ exterminator   _____ locksmith

_____ cockroach   _____ fuse box   _____ plumber

_____ electrician   _____ lock   __1__ repairperson

B Listen and check your answers. Then practice the words with a partner.

1-42

C Complete the paragraph with the words from 2A. Check your work with a partner.

My new home has a lot of problems, but soon it will be problem-free! Inside, the

<u>electrician</u> is checking the fuse box. The _____ is in the kitchen. He's replacing a
   1   2

leaking pipe. And there's a _____ in the bedroom. She's repairing the closet door.
                              3

Outside, the _____ is fixing the front door. The _____ is replacing a broken
                 4   5

window. And the _____ is getting rid of the mice and cockroaches.
                  6

D Think about it. Ask and answer the questions with your classmates.

1. Which household repairs can you do?
2. Which repairs are difficult for landlords to make? Why?

▶▶ **TEST YOURSELF**

Copy the chart in your notebook. Write six household
problems and the correct repairperson for each one.

Problem	Repairperson

1 Prepare to write

A Read the ad. Which abbreviations do you know? Complete the sentences.

security deposit	bathroom	evenings
manager	month	~~large~~

FOR RENT:

lg sunny 2BR 1BA apt, nr school and mall, $1,000/mo. $500 sec. dep.
Call mgr. eves 555-5151

1. It's a __large__ apartment with two bedrooms and one _____ .
2. The rent is $1,000 a _____ , and the _____ is $500.
3. For information, call the _____ at 555-5151 in the _____ .

B Look at the pictures. Listen to the story.

1-43

Teresa's apartment   Teresa's dream home

C Listen again and read Teresa's paragraph about her dream home.

1-43

My Dream Home

I am looking for a new apartment. Right now, my apartment has only one bedroom, but I need an apartment with two bedrooms. My apartment now is too dark, and the windows are small. There is a lot of noise. I want a larger, sunnier apartment in a quieter neighborhood. This street is also very dangerous. I want to live on a safer street. Finally, I want to live closer to my children's school and not far from the park.

WRITER'S NOTE
Use *finally* to introduce the last point in a list.

D Check your understanding. Circle the correct words.

1. Teresa is looking for a new (house / apartment).
2. Teresa's dream home has (one / two) bedrooms.
3. Her home right now is (sunny / noisy).
4. Her dream home is (near / far from) the park.

E Listen to Anya describe her dream home. Circle the things she wants.

1. Number of bedrooms: 2   3   4
2. Number of bathrooms: 1   2   3
3. Near: mall   school   bus stop
4. Rent: $900 $1,200 $2,500

F Compare answers with your partner. Listen again and check your work.

2 Plan

A Complete the information about your dream home.

> # Oakley Realty makes your dreams come true!
> # Tell us about your dream home.
>
> ☐ house ☐ apartment ☐ condo _____ # of bedrooms _____ # of bathrooms
> ☐ garage ☐ family room ☐ backyard ☐ pool
> **Near:**
> ☐ school ☐ supermarket ☐ shopping ☐ mall ☐ train or bus stop ☐ park

B Role-play a conversation between a realtor and a homebuyer. Work with a partner. Use your own ideas.

A: *Tell me about your dream home. What kind of home are you looking for?*

B: *I want a big house with four bedrooms and a pool in the backyard.*

3 Write

A Write a description of your dream home. Use your information from 2A.

> My Dream Home
>
> My dream home is _____ . I need _____ bedrooms with _____ bathrooms.
> I want to have a large _____ and a _____ . My dream home will be in a _____
> neighborhood. Finally, I also want to live near a _____ and not far from a _____ .

B Share your writing. Read your description to a partner.

▶▶ TEST YOURSELF

Complete the following sentences. Share your responses with your teacher.

1. After this writing lesson, I can…   2. I need more help with…

1 Explore the comparative

A Look at the floor plans. Then listen and read about the apartments. What do you think? Which apartment is better?

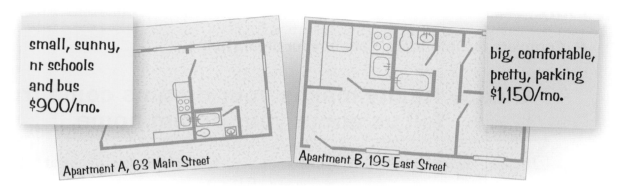

small, sunny, nr schools and bus $900/mo.

Apartment A, 63 Main Street

big, comfortable, pretty, parking $1,150/mo.

Apartment B, 195 East Street

Apartment A is smaller and cheaper than apartment B. It's near schools and the bus, so it's more convenient. Apartment A is very sunny. Apartment B is bigger and more comfortable. It's also a very pretty apartment, but it's more expensive.

B Analyze the sentences in 1A. Underline the adjectives. Which adjectives end in *-er*? Which adjectives follow *more*? What do you notice about them?

C Study the grammar. Read the chart.

The Comparative			
	Adjective	**Comparative**	**Notes**
One syllable	small large big	smaller larger bigger	Add *-er* or *-r*. For words like *big* and *hot*, double the final consonant.
Ending in *-y*	sunny	sunnier	Change *y* to *i* and add *-er*.
Two or more syllables	convenient	more convenient	Put *more* in front of the adjective.
Irregular forms	good bad	better worse	

D Work with a partner. Take turns comparing apartment A and apartment B. Use the words in the grammar chart.

A: Apartment A is more convenient than apartment B.

B: Apartment B is larger than apartment A.

E Work with a partner. Write a sentence for each rule in the 1C chart. Share your sentences with the class.

2 Practice: ask and answer questions with *which*

🔊
1-46

A Study the chart. Listen and repeat the questions and answers.

Questions with *which*
Which is better, apartment A or apartment B?
Which apartment is better, A or B?

Answers
Apartment A is better than apartment B.
Apartment A is better.

B Check your understanding. Complete the questions using the comparative.

1. Which is usually _cheaper_ , an apartment or a house? (cheap)

   I think an apartment is usually cheaper than a house .

2. Which place is _____ , a small town or a big city? (safe)

   _____

3. Which is _____ , a car or a bicycle? (dangerous)

   _____

4. Which city is _____ , New York or San Francisco? (expensive)

   _____

C Write three questions about places in your city. Ask your classmates.

   A: *Which is cheaper, Ben's Restaurant or Tony's Café?*

   B: *I think Ben's Restaurant is cheaper.*

3 Practice: adverbs of degree with comparatives

A Study the grammar. Look at the diagram and make sentences using the chart.

Adverbs of degree: *much, a lot, a little, a bit*				
Apartment A	is	a little / a bit	more expensive	than	Apartment B.
House B		much / a lot	cheaper		House A.

Apartment A
$1,500 per month

Apartment B
$1,450 per month

House A
$4,000 per month

House B
$1,200 per month

B Complete the sentences below with an adverb of degree and a comparative adjective. Compare opinions with a partner.

1. A farm is _much quieter_ than a house in the city. (quiet)

2. An apartment is _____ to repair than a house. (easy)

3. Rents in a big city are _____ than in a small city. (expensive)

4. Neighborhoods in a small town are _____ than in a big city. (safe)

5. Public transportation in a city is _____ than in the country. (convenient)

C Work with a partner. Look at the pictures. Ask questions to compare them. Use adverbs of degree and the words in the box.

large	small
safe	dangerous
cheap	expensive
sunny	dark
good	bad

$2,300/month $1,200/month

$4,500 $25,000

A: *Which house is larger?*

B: *The first house is much larger.*

A: *Yes. I think it is much larger.*

D Write sentences in your notebook about the pictures.

The first house is much larger than the second house.

4 Practice: questions and answers with the comparative

A Read the questions. Write your answers in your notebook. Use the words from 3C and your own ideas.

1. Which is better, a new house or an old house? Why?
2. Which is worse, a small house or a large apartment? Why?
3. Which is better, an apartment on the first floor or on the top floor? Why?

B Talk to a partner. Ask and answer the questions in 4A.

A: *Which is better, a new house or an old house?*

B: *I think a new house is better. It's much more comfortable.*

C Share your answers with your classmates.

▶▶TEST YOURSELF

Write three sentences about your partner's opinions from 4B.

My partner thinks a new house is much more comfortable than an old house.

1 Listen to learn: asking about an apartment

A Read the ad. Work with a partner. Ask and answer the questions.

1. How many bedrooms does the apartment have?
2. Is it near a school?
3. How much is the rent?
4. Is there a security deposit?
5. Are utilities included?

FOR RENT:
Cozy 1BR, 1BA apt, top floor, nr sch, $800/mo. $650 sec. dep. Parking space. Util. incl. Call 219-555-4609

B Listen. What is Sharon asking about?

1-47

C Listen again. Complete the notes.

1-47

114 Maple St.

Rent: _____

Deposit: _____

Utilities included:

Yes / No

Available: _____

15 Center St.

Rent: _____

Deposit: _____

Utilities included:

Yes / No

Available: _____

198 Second Ave.

Rent: _____

Deposit: _____

Utilities included:

Yes / No

Available: _____

2 Practice your pronunciation

A Listen to the falling and rising intonation. Then listen again and repeat.

1-48

Information questions

How much is the rent? ↘

When is it available? ↘

Yes/no questions

Is there a security deposit? ↗

Are pets allowed? ↗

B Read the questions. Check (✔) *Falling* or *Rising*. Then listen and check your answers.

1-49

	Falling ↘	Rising ↗
1. When can I see it?		
2. Is there a garage?		
3. How much is the rent?		
4. Does it include utilities?		

C Talk to a partner. Practice the questions. Use falling and rising intonation.

3 Practice asking about apartment regulations

 A Listen and read the conversation. Which regulation does Sharon ask about?

1-50

Sharon: Hello. I'm calling about the apartment. How much is the rent?

Manager: It's $900 a month plus utilities.

Sharon: Is there a security deposit?

Manager: Yes, there is, but it's not too bad. It's $450.

Sharon: Are pets allowed?

Manager: I'm sorry, but they aren't.

Sharon: When will the apartment be available?

Manager: It'll be available on March 1st. It's a very nice apartment.

B Listen and mark the correct answers.

1-51

1. a. Yes, it is.   b. No, it isn't.   3. a. Yes, they are.   b. No, they aren't.

2. a. Yes, they are.   b. No, they aren't.   4. a. Yes, it is.   b. No, it isn't.

C Think about the grammar. Look at the conversation and answer the questions.

1. How do you form questions with *be allowed*?

2. When do you use *is + allowed* or *are + allowed*?

D Study the grammar. Listen and repeat.

1-52

Yes/no questions with *be + allowed*			Short answers	
Is	smoking	allowed?	Yes, it is.	No, it isn't.
Are	pets		Yes, they are.	No, they aren't.

E Talk to a partner. Ask and answer questions about the apartment regulations. Add your own ideas.

A: *Are dogs allowed?*   A: *Are cats allowed?*

B: *No, they aren't.*   B: *Yes, they are.*

CONDO REGULATIONS

✓ **Pets** — only cats

✓ **Bicycles** — only in storage area

✗ **No smoking**

✗ **Parties** — no loud music after 10 p.m.

✓ **Basement storage**

✓ **Backyard** — open to all residents, so please keep it tidy!

4 Make conversation: asking about an apartment

A Work with a partner. Make a new conversation.

A: Hello. I'm calling about the apartment. How much is the _____ ?

B: It's _____ a month plus utilities.

A: Is there a _____ ?

B: Yes, there is. It's _____ .

A: _____ allowed?

B: I'm sorry, but they aren't.

A: When is the apartment available?

B: It's available on _____ . It's a very nice apartment.

B Present your conversation to another pair. Observe their conversation.

AT WORK ▶ Asking about regulations

A Listen to different ways to ask about regulations at work.

Suzanna:	Can I ask about workplace regulations?
HR manager:	Yes, of course. What do you want to know?
Suzanna:	Can we park in front of the building?
HR manager:	No, but you can park in the staff parking lot behind the building.
Suzanna:	Are jeans and T-shirts allowed?
HR manager:	It's OK to wear T-shirts, but jeans aren't allowed.
Suzanna:	Can we check our personal email at work?
HR manager:	Yes, that's fine. But do it on your break or during lunch!

1-53

Human Resources manager

B Talk to a partner. Practice the conversation in A. Take turns asking about regulations at work and in school.

C Think about it. Ask and answer the questions with a partner.

1. Who are the people in A? Where are they? Do they know each other?

2. Look at the Need Help box. Which questions are more formal or more informal?

3. What are some other situations when you need to ask about regulations?

NEED HELP?

Is it OK to…?

Do we need to…?

Are we allowed to…?

▶▶ TEST YOURSELF

Act out this situation with a classmate. Take turns with each role.

New employee: Ask about the regulations in your workplace.
HR manager: Answer the questions.

1 Build reading strategies

A Complete the paragraph with words from the box. Write definitions for the words in blue. Check them in your dictionary.

utilities	share	rent	own

    Landlords _____ apartments or other rentals, such as houses or condos.
Tenants pay _____ to the landlord. They also pay for the gas,
electricity, and other _____ . Roommates usually _____ the rent
and utility bills.

B Where do you look for information about finding an apartment? Circle your answers.

newspaper / the Internet / community center / supermarket / friends

C Read the article. Who is the audience for this article? How do you know?

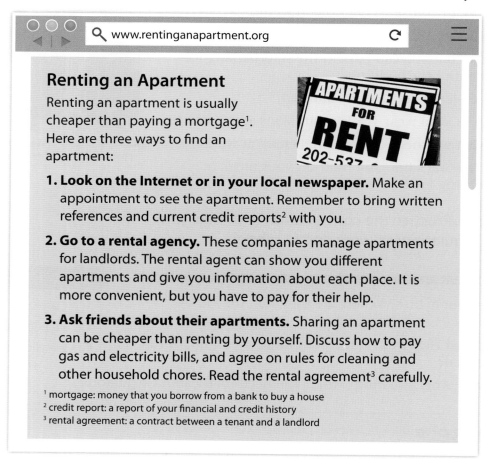

READER'S NOTE
Identify the purpose of the text. Who is it for? What is the writer's purpose?

Renting an Apartment

Renting an apartment is usually cheaper than paying a mortgage[1]. Here are three ways to find an apartment:

1. **Look on the Internet or in your local newspaper.** Make an appointment to see the apartment. Remember to bring written references and current credit reports[2] with you.

2. **Go to a rental agency.** These companies manage apartments for landlords. The rental agent can show you different apartments and give you information about each place. It is more convenient, but you have to pay for their help.

3. **Ask friends about their apartments.** Sharing an apartment can be cheaper than renting by yourself. Discuss how to pay gas and electricity bills, and agree on rules for cleaning and other household chores. Read the rental agreement[3] carefully.

[1] mortgage: money that you borrow from a bank to buy a house
[2] credit report: a report of your financial and credit history
[3] rental agreement: a contract between a tenant and a landlord

 D Listen and read the article again.
1-54

E **Read the questions. Fill in the bubble next to the correct answer.**

1. What is the main topic of the article?
   - (a) how to rent an apartment
   - (b) how to find an apartment to rent
   - (c) how to choose the best apartment

2. What does the article say about getting a mortgage?
   - (a) It's cheaper than renting.
   - (b) It's more difficult than renting.
   - (c) It's more expensive than renting.

3. Why is a rental agency more expensive?
   - (a) They charge a fee.
   - (b) They work for the landlord.
   - (c) They only rent expensive homes.

4. According to the article, what do you need to discuss with a roommate?
   - (a) how to make a profit
   - (b) how to save money
   - (c) how to pay for utilities

F **Complete the sentences. Use the words in the box.**

utilities	landlord	roommate	agreement

1. I need to ask my _____ about repairing the window.
2. I signed a rental _____ for one year.
3. It's sometimes cheaper to share the rent with a _____ .
4. Are _____ included in your rent?

2 Read a rental agreement

A **Read the rental agreement. Ask and answer the questions with a partner.**

1. Where will Jake Wilson live?
2. Who is the landlord?
3. What is Jake's rent for one month?
4. Which utilities are included in the rent?

B **Which item in the rental agreement is also mentioned in the reading passage?**

RENTAL AGREEMENT

LANDLORD Mr. Ken Mason   TENANT Mr. Jake Wilson
PROPERTY ADDRESS: 1573 New Street, Jackson, Mississippi 39202

1. RENTAL AMOUNT: TENANT agrees to pay LANDLORD the sum of $850 per month starting on 10/01/18 .

2. SECURITY DEPOSIT: TENANT will deposit with landlord the sum of $1,200 as a security deposit.

3. INITIAL PAYMENT: TENANT will pay the first month rent of $850 and the security deposit in the amount of $1,200 for a total of $2,050 .

4. UTILITIES: TENANT will pay for all utilities except: heating .

5. RULES: TENANT will agree to all apartment rules and regulations concerning pets, smoking, noise, and parking.

| K. Mason | LANDLORD/AGENT | 9/31/18 | DATE |
| J. Wilson | TENANT | 9/31/18 | DATE |

 BRING IT TO LIFE

Find information about regulations in your apartment building or an apartment building near your school. Talk about the information with your class.

A Work with a team. Discuss and compare the different places to live. What are the good points of each type of place? What are the possible problems?

condo

farm

mobile home

nursing home

B Work with your team. Complete the chart with your answers from A.

	Apartment	Condo	Farm	Mobile home	Nursing home
comfortable					
convenient					
expensive					
cheap					
easy to take care of					
friendly					

C Work with your team to write a summary of your opinions. Present your team's opinions to the class.

Most people in our group think that condos and rental apartments are more comfortable than mobile homes. We think that mobile homes are cheaper to rent, but condos are usually larger and also safer.

D Work with your team. You are the landlords of an old house. The house has a lot of problems. Decide which ones you can solve and which ones need a repairperson. Write the team member's name or the type of repairperson.

1. The kitchen stove is dirty. _____

2. There is a hole in the living room wall. _____

3. There are mice in the basement. _____

4. The bathroom needs a new sink. _____

5. The fuse box is very old. _____

6. The fence is broken. _____

7. The grass in the backyard is very long. _____

E **Report to the class with a summary of which jobs you will do and who you will call for repairs.**

F **Work with your team. Choose one person to be the secretary. You are now tenants in the house in D. Write a note to your landlord about one of the problems. Share your note with your classmates.**

> Dear Mr. Mason,
>
> I am writing about a problem in my house. There is a cracked window, and it's dangerous. Could you please ask a repairperson to fix the window as soon as possible? Thank you.
>
> Sincerely,
>
> Hilde Lopez

PROBLEM SOLVING

1-55

A **Listen and read about Dan and Lia.**

> Dan and Lia are renting an apartment in the city. It is expensive. They want to buy a house, but houses in the city are more expensive than apartments. Houses in the small town of Riverville are a little cheaper.
>
> Right now Dan and Lia don't have the money for a house in the city. But they have the money for a house in Riverville. Lia can find a job in Riverville, but Dan works in the city. Now he takes the bus to work and it only takes 15 minutes. From Riverville, he will have to commute two hours by car to work every day.

B **Work with your classmates. Answer the questions.**

1. What is Dan and Lia's problem?
2. What should they do? Think of two or three solutions to their problem.

UNIT

4 Looking for Work

A LOOK AT
- Jobs and job applications
- Simple past
- Talking about job skills

LESSON 1 VOCABULARY

1 Learn about job applications

A Show what you know. Give an example for each section of the job application.

1. personal information
2. job skills
3. interests
4. education
5. employment history
6. references

APPLICATION FOR EMPLOYMENT

① NAME (LAST, FIRST, MIDDLE INITIAL):
Sousa, Katia M.

ADDRESS (STREET, CITY, STATE):
387 Jensen Street, Tampa, FL

HOME PHONE:
(813) 555-5005

② SKILLS:
computers, Portuguese

③ HOBBIES:
cooking, volunteer work

④ NAME AND LOCATION OF SCHOOL:
County Community College, Tampa, FL

NAME OF EMPLOYER	POSITION	DATES OF EMPLOYMENT ⑤
Sam's Supermarket	Assistant Manager	2015–present
Fran's Pizza Restaurant	Server	2012–2014

⑥ NAME AND CONTACT INFORMATION

Sam Giannini, Employer
(813) 555-5500
sam@internet.us

Beth Marcello, Teacher
(813) 555-2213
bmarcello@internet.us

B Listen and look at the job application. Katia wants to be a supermarket manager.
1-56 What sections of the application will help her most?

C Listen and repeat the words from 1A.
1-57

D Write the vocabulary. Look at the job application. Complete the sentences.

1. Katia writes the name of her manager at Sam's in the ___references___ section.
2. Katia writes things she is good at in the _____ section.
3. The name of Katia's college goes in the _____ section.
4. Katia's name and address are in the _____ section.
5. Katia's last job is in the _____ section.
6. Katia writes her free-time activities in the _____ section.

E Ask your partner about each of the sections in 1B.

A: *What do you write in the personal information section?*

B: *You write your name, address, and phone number.*

2 Talk about jobs

A Work with your classmates. Match the words with the pictures.

_____ accountant   _____ job applicant   _____ mover

_____ chef   __1__ job counselor   _____ sales clerk

_____ computer programmer _____ mail carrier   _____ veterinarian

 B Listen and check your answers. Repeat the name of each job.
1-58   Practice the words with a partner.

C Talk about the people in 2A. Use the phrases in the box.

A: What does a veterinarian do?

B: She takes care of sick animals.

brings furniture to a new home	helps people find a job
cooks food in a restaurant	helps people with taxes
delivers mail	takes care of sick animals
helps customers in a store	writes computer programs

D Think about it. Ask and answer the questions with your classmates.

1. Which of the jobs on this page are interesting to you? Why?

2. Which is more important for a job, education or experience? Explain.

3. Analyze the job descriptions in 2C. Which jobs require more education or training than other jobs? Which jobs have on-the-job training?

▶▶**TEST YOURSELF**

Copy the chart in your notebook. Write your information in each section.

Education	Employment history	Job skills

1 Prepare to write

A Look at the pictures. What is Adam doing in each picture? How does he feel?

B Look at the pictures. Listen to the story.
1-59

C Listen again and read the story.
1-59

Looking for a Job

I'm looking for a full-time job, and I go to job interviews every week. Before the interview, I usually look on the Internet for information about the company. Then I write some questions to ask in the interview. I always wear a suit and a tie, and I'm careful not to be late.

During the interview, I sometimes feel nervous. It's hard for me to smile and make eye contact. It's a good thing I can look at my notes! At the end of the interview, I always shake hands with the interviewer and say thank you.

I had an interview last week. I was a little worried, and I wasn't very confident, but I answered all the questions. After the interview, I emailed the company to say thank you. I hope I'll get the job!

> **WRITER'S NOTE**
> **Use time words to show sequence.**
>
> Before the interview…
>
> During the interview…
>
> After the interview…

D Check your understanding. Check (✔) the three mistakes Adam makes at job interviews.

☐ 1. He writes questions for the job interview.
☐ 2. He doesn't look at the interviewer.
☐ 3. He doesn't smile very much.
☐ 4. He wears nice clothes.
☐ 5. He's not confident.
☐ 6. He doesn't answer the questions.

E Discuss the questions with your class.

1. What kind of advice can you give to Adam?

2. What are some ways to reduce stress in a job interview?

F Read the job ad. Match the abbreviations with the words below.

_____ references

_____ experience

_____ immediately

_____ part-time

Customer sales associate wanted

(1) p/t 9 a.m–1:00 p.m.

(2) exp. not necessary, training provided

(3) written refs. required

(4) start immed.

G Listen to two job interviews. Complete the chart.

1-60

	Experience	Job skills	Confident or nervous?
Rick			
Alexa			

H Discuss with the class. Which person is better for the job? Why?

2 Plan

Think about a recent interview or important event. Copy and complete this chart in your notebook. Then work with a partner. Help each other add details to your charts.

| Before | | During | | After |

3 Write

A Describe what you usually do before, during, and after a job interview or other important event.

Before an interview, I usually _____ and _____ .

I put on a _____ and _____ .

During the interview, I usually _____ . I never _____ .

After my interview, I _____ and _____ . I usually feel _____ .

NEED HELP?

✔	✘
confident	worried
relaxed	nervous
cheerful	stressed

B Share your work with a partner. Say one thing you like about your partner's description. Discuss some different ideas to improve your job interviews.

▶▶ TEST YOURSELF

Complete the following sentences. Share your responses with your teacher.

1. After this writing lesson, I can…   2. I need more help with…

LESSON 3 GRAMMAR

1 Explore the simple past

A Listen and read about Katia. Did she work and study at the same time?

1-61

> In 2012, Katia Sousa worked at Fran's Pizza Restaurant. Every evening, she attended County Community College and studied Business Administration and English. She graduated in 2015. Then she worked at Sam's Supermarket as an assistant manager. Last week, she applied for a job at State Bank.

B Analyze the grammar in 1A. Underline the verbs in the simple past. What is the same about them?

C Study the grammar. Read the charts.

The simple past

Affirmative statements

I			We			Regular verbs
You	worked	at Sam's.	You	worked	at Sam's.	work → worked
He			They			graduate → graduated
She						apply → applied

Negative statements

I			We		
You	didn't work	at Sam's.	You	didn't work	at Sam's.
He			They		
She					

D Work with the grammar. Complete the sentences. Use the simple past of the verbs in parentheses.

1. Katia __worked__ at Sam's Supermarket in 2016. (work)
2. She _____ County Community College. (attend)
3. She _____ business and English. (study)
4. She _didn't study_ Portuguese. (not study)
5. She _____ in 2010. (not graduate)
6. She _____ for a job in a hotel. (not apply)

SPELLING NOTE

For verbs that end in a consonant + *y*, change *y* to *i* and add *-ed*.
study → studied
apply → applied

E Work with a partner. Make sentences using the chart.

2 Practice: the simple past

A Read Katia's to-do list. What did Katia do after her job interview yesterday?

> Katia's To-Do List
> ✗ pick up dry cleaning
> ✗ return books to the library
> ✔ call Nicole
> ✔ cook dinner
> ✔ bake cookies
> ✗ finish her homework

B Listen to the sentences about Katia. Circle *True* or *False*.

1-62

1. True False   4. True   False

2. True False   5. True   False

3. True False   6. True   False

C Look at the to-do list in 2A. Complete the paragraph about Katia. Use the simple past of the verbs in the box.

ask	bake	call	cook	pick	reply	return	walk

After her job interview yesterday, Katia _____ home. She _____ up her dry
                                                        1   2
cleaning and she _____ her library books because the dry cleaner's and the library
                        3
were closed. At home, she _____ her best friend, Nicole. "How was your interview?"
                                    4
Nicole _____ . "Oh, not too bad!" _____ Katia. Then she _____
            5   6   7
dinner for her family and _____ some cookies for her daughter. At the end of the day,
                                  8
she was really tired.

D Work with a partner. Take turns making true or false statements about Katia.

A: *Katia was really tired.*

B: *That's true. Katia baked bread.*

A: *That's false. She baked cookies. Katia…*

3 Practice: information questions in the simple past

🔊 1-63 **A** Study the grammar. Listen and repeat the conversations.

Information questions		
A: What time did you start work yesterday? **B:** I started work at 8:00 a.m.	**A:** Who did she call yesterday? **B:** She called her best friend.	**A:** How long did they talk on the phone? **B:** They talked for about twenty minutes.

B Complete the simple past questions. Use the words in parentheses.

1. What time <u>did he start work</u> yesterday? (he, start work)
2. Who _____ after work yesterday? (they, visit)
3. When _____ from high school? (she, graduate)
4. How long _____ in Miami? (you, live)

C Work with the grammar. Write the questions.

1. <u>What did she watch on TV last night</u> ? She watched a movie on TV last night.
2. _____ ? I visited my aunt and uncle last weekend.
3. _____ ? We stayed in the library for two hours.
4. _____ ? They studied Spanish last year.
5. _____ ? He worked in a hospital for three years.

> **GRAMMAR NOTE**
>
> Use **for** with periods of time.
> I lived in Miami **for** three years.
> We talked **for** ten minutes.

4 Talk about past events in your life

A Write questions about yesterday.

1. start work or school   <u>What time did you start work yesterday?</u>
2. finish work or school   _____
3. call on the phone   _____
4. watch on TV   _____
5. study English   _____

B Work with a partner. Ask and answer the questions in 4A. Then write sentences about what your partner did yesterday.

Carmen started work at 8:00 a.m.

▶▶ **TEST YOURSELF**

Write three sentences about yesterday, last week, and last year. Use these verbs: *live, work, study.*

1 Listen to learn: job interviews

A Look at the pictures in 1B. What are their jobs? What skills do they need?

B Listen to three conversations. Match the conversations with the jobs.

1-64

_____ _____ _____

C Listen again. Answer the questions.

1-64

1. What did they do in their last jobs?

2. What are they good at? (What can they do well?)

2 Practice your pronunciation

A Listen to the verbs in the simple present and simple past. How many syllables are there in each verb?

1-65

NEED HELP?
Regular verbs that end in the sound *t* or *d* have an extra syllable in the simple past. For example, *wanted* sounds like *wan-ted*.

1. talk   talked   3. count   counted

2. answer   answered   4. want   wanted

B Listen to the simple present and simple past of the verbs. How many syllables are there in the simple past? Circle 1 or 2.

1-66

1. clean   cleaned   1   2

2. need   needed   1   2

3. wait   waited   1   2

4. fix   fixed   1   2

5. check   checked   1   2

6. paint   painted   1   2

C Listen again and repeat.

1-66

D Read the sentences to a partner.

1. I cleaned the car.

2. She wanted a new job.

3. The carpenter fixed the door.

4. He painted the house in 2017.

3 Practice job interview questions

 A Listen and read the conversation.

1-67

Interviewer:	Tell me about your education.
Mark:	I graduated last June with an AS degree.
Interviewer:	What did you study?
Mark:	I studied computer programming.
Interviewer:	What kind of experience do you have?
Mark:	I worked for the Energy Electrical Company. I was a clerk.
Interviewer:	How long did you work there?
Mark:	For six months.
Interviewer:	What kind of job skills do you have?
Mark:	I'm an effective problem solver. I work carefully. And I speak Spanish fluently.
Interviewer:	Do you have any references?
Mark:	Yes, I do. You can call my manager at Energy Electrical, Joe Russo.

 B Listen and mark the answers to the questions.

1-68

1. a. He graduated from college.   b. He worked in an office.

2. a. for six months   b. for six years

3. a. talking to people   b. solving problems and speaking Spanish

4. a. his math teacher   b. his manager

C Think about the grammar. Look at the conversation and answer the questions.

1. Underline the questions about the past.

2. Which words describe *how* someone does something?

D Study the grammar. Listen and repeat.

1-69

Adjectives	Adverbs
She is a **careful** driver.	She drives **carefully**.
He is a **slow** writer.	He writes **slowly**.
They are **quick** workers.	They work **quickly**.
Your work was **good**.	You did this work **well**.

GRAMMAR NOTE

Adverbs of manner describe **how** someone does an activity. To make adverbs of manner, add *-ly* to an adjective. One exception is *good*. The adverb for *good* is *well*.

E Write three questions. Choose adjectives or adverbs from the chart. Then ask and answer the questions with a partner.

A: *Do you drive your car carefully?*

B: *Yes, I do. / No. I don't drive a car, but I ride my bicycle carefully!*

4 Make conversation: talking about your job skills

A Work with a partner. Make a new conversation.

A: Tell me about your education. What did you study?

B: I _____ . I _____ .

A: What kind of experience do you have?

B: I worked at _____ .

A: How long did you work there?

B: _____ .

A: What kind of job skills do you have?

B: Well, I _____ . And I can _____ .

A: Do you have any references?

B: Yes, I do. You can call _____ .

NEED HELP?

Job skills
talking with people
writing emails
answering the phone
solving problems

B Present your conversation to another pair. Observe their conversation. What simple past verbs did they use?

AT WORK ▶ Evaluate a job interview

🔊 1-70 **A** Listen and evaluate the interview. Complete the checklist.

- ☐ talked about her job skills
- ☐ answered questions clearly
- ☐ asked some questions about the job
- ☐ didn't sound nervous
- ☐ thanked the interviewer
- ☐ greeted the interviewer politely
- ☐ sounded cheerful and upbeat
- ☐ described her job experience

Tell me about your education.

I finished high school and I studied computers.

Interviewer

Sara

B Think about your last job interview. Ask and answer the questions with a partner.

1. How did you perform in the interview? Were you nervous or confident?

2. What questions did the interviewer ask? What questions did you ask?

3. What could you improve next time?

▶▶ **TEST YOURSELF**

Act out this situation with a classmate. Take turns with each role.

Interviewer: You are looking for an employee with computer skills and telephone skills. Ask questions to help you make a decision.

Interviewee: You want the job very much. Answer the interviewer's questions.

ACADEMIC

1 Build reading strategies

A Read the definitions. Are these words nouns, adjectives, or verbs?
Look them up in a dictionary. Find an example sentence for each word.

average: typical, normal, common

employer: someone who gives you a job

salary: money you get for your work

B Think about it. What are some reasons people change their careers?
Think of some examples from your friends or family. Tell your partner.

My brother changed his job because he got married.

C Read the article. Who do you think this website is for?

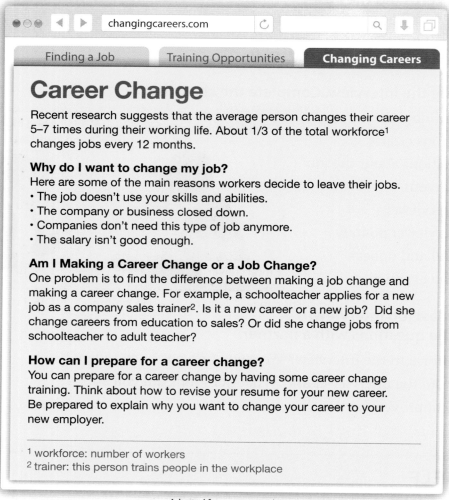

changingcareers.com

| Finding a Job | Training Opportunities | **Changing Careers** |

Career Change

Recent research suggests that the average person changes their career
5–7 times during their working life. About 1/3 of the total workforce[1]
changes jobs every 12 months.

Why do I want to change my job?
Here are some of the main reasons workers decide to leave their jobs.
• The job doesn't use your skills and abilities.
• The company or business closed down.
• Companies don't need this type of job anymore.
• The salary isn't good enough.

Am I Making a Career Change or a Job Change?
One problem is to find the difference between making a job change and
making a career change. For example, a schoolteacher applies for a new
job as a company sales trainer[2]. Is it a new career or a new job? Did she
change careers from education to sales? Or did she change jobs from
schoolteacher to adult teacher?

How can I prepare for a career change?
You can prepare for a career change by having some career change
training. Think about how to revise your resume for your new career.
Be prepared to explain why you want to change your career to your
new employer.

---
[1] workforce: number of workers
[2] trainer: this person trains people in the workplace

Adapted from: *careers-advice-online.com; U.S. Department of Labor*

READER'S NOTE
The navigation bar at
the top of the website
helps to tell you where
you are and what other
information is available
on the website.

D Listen and read the article again. How often do people change careers?

1-71

E **Read the questions. Fill in the bubble next to the correct answer.**

1. Read the headings. Who does "I" refer to?
   (a) the reader
   (b) the writer
   (c) an unknown person

2. What does the article say about changing careers?
   (a) Most people change careers every year.
   (b) Changing careers is very unusual.
   (c) You need to train for a new career.

3. What does the example of the schoolteacher show?
   (a) Some people change jobs, but not careers.
   (b) It isn't easy to change careers.
   (c) Some people cannot change jobs.

4. What kind of information is **not** on this website?
   (a) how to find job training
   (b) how to look for jobs
   (c) how to write a resume

F **Complete the sentences. Use the words in the box.**

average	employer	salary	trainer

1. Sam's _____ offered him a great promotion.

2. He'll earn a _____ of $3,000 a month as an administrative assistant.

3. Yesterday at work, a _____ showed him how to make spreadsheets.

4. The _____ administrative assistant earns $18 an hour.

2 Read a job training chart

A **Read the chart. Ask and answer questions about the chart.**

Position	Education/Training	Average salary
Mail carrier	High school diploma or GED certificate + 1 year on-the-job training	$56,790 per year
Nursing assistant	Nurse training certificate + 1 year on-the-job training	$25,710 per year
Veterinary assistant	Associate's degree + 1–2 years on-the-job training	$24,360 per year
Computer programmer	Bachelor's degree + 2 years on-the-job training	$79,530 per year

Source: *U.S. Department of Labor*

B **Think about it. Talk about these questions with your classmates.**

1. What is important to you in a job? A good salary? Interesting work? Friendly co-workers?

2. What is the most important reason to change jobs? Explain.

BRING IT TO LIFE

Talk to two friends or family members about their career plans. Tell your classmates.

A Work with a team. Look at the picture of a job fair. Answer the questions.

1. Who are the people standing in front of the tables? Why are they here?
2. Who are the people sitting and standing behind the tables?
3. What do you think the woman in the blue hijab is asking? How do you know?
4. What kind of information can the people behind the tables give?
5. What questions are people asking?
6. Is this a good way to find out about careers? Why or why not?
7. What are some other ways to find out about careers?

B Complete the conversation. Use the simple past of the verbs in the box.

answer	help	not stay	want	work	work

A: How long _____ you _____ at ABC Corporation?

B: I _____ there for three years.

A: Tell me about your work.

B: I _____ the phone and _____ customers.

A: And why _____ you _____ with the company?

B: Because I _____ a better career and a better salary.

C Look at the picture in A. Write a conversation of 6–8 lines between two people in the picture. Talk about job skills, training, and experience.

D Work with two or three classmates. Act out your conversation for the class.

A: *Good morning. I'm Sara Abadi. Can you tell me a little about your company?*

B: *Of course, Sara. At Franklin, we install and repair electrical systems in homes and businesses.*

E ABC Corp. has four jobs available. Match the job titles to the job skills needed.

_____ 1. a chef for the cafeteria

_____ 2. a forklift driver to work in the warehouse

_____ 3. a graphic designer in the design department

_____ 4. a salesperson

a. good at talking with people and communicating

b. good at preparing food carefully and safely

c. good at moving heavy objects

d. good at thinking of new ideas and solving technical problems

F Work with a team. What other skills are necessary for each job in E? Make a list.

G Interview your teammates. What job skills did they learn in the last three years? Write their answers in the chart.

Name	Job skills
Martin	He typed emails. He learned to drive a truck.

H Write a summary of your team's skills.

The people in our team have a variety of different skills. Three of us can speak Spanish and Portuguese really well, and one person speaks Russian. Three of us are very good at math, and four people are good with computers.

PROBLEM SOLVING AT WORK

A Listen and read about Jin. What is the problem?

1-72

Jin is married and has two young children. He works as a sales clerk in a large computer store. He enjoys his job because he talks to people and helps them choose the right computer for their job or for home. But there aren't many opportunities to develop his career. He feels frustrated and wants to change his job, but he doesn't know where to start.

B Work with your classmates. Answer the questions.

1. What is Jin's problem?

2. What can he do? Think of two or three solutions to his problem.

UNIT

5 On the Job

A LOOK AT
- Pay stubs and the workplace
- *Might* and *should*
- Requesting a schedule change

LESSON 1 VOCABULARY

1 Learn about reading a pay stub

A Show what you know. Circle the words you know.

1. pay period
2. hourly rate
3. gross pay
4. deductions
5. net pay
6. federal tax
7. Medicare
8. Social Security

(1) PAY PERIOD

01/10/18–01/16/18

Mills Brothers Company

EMPLOYEE NAME	SSN	EMPLOYEE NUMBER
Pablo Ramirez	123-45-6789	0005643

EARNINGS

Hours	28	
(2) Hourly rate	$15.25	
(3) — Gross pay		$427.00
(4) Deductions		- $101.40
(5) Net pay		$325.60

DEDUCTIONS

State tax	$20.10
(6) Federal tax	$48.64
(7) — Medicare	$ 6.19
(8) Social Security	$26.47
Total deductions	$101.40

B Listen and look at the pay stub. How often does Pablo get paid?
2-02

C Listen and repeat the words from 1A.
2-03

D Write the vocabulary. Look at the pay stub. Complete the sentences.

1. Pablo's net pay is his gross pay minus the __deductions__ .
2. Pablo's employer deducted $26.47 for _____ .
3. Pablo's _____ is $15.25 per hour.
4. The deduction for _____ is $48.64.
5. Pablo's _____ for this week is $427.
6. This _____ is one week.
7. Pablo paid $6.19 for _____ .
8. Pablo's _____ is $325.60.

E Talk to a partner. Ask and answer the questions.

1. What are the dates for this pay period?
2. How many deductions are there?

2 Talk about workplace equipment

A Work with your classmates. Match the words with the picture.
Which other items can you name?

_____ printer   _____ keyboard   _____ hand cart

_____ water cooler   _____ monitor   __1__ time clock

_____ forklift   _____ photocopier   _____ file cabinet

B Listen and check your answers.

2-04

C Talk to a partner. Ask and answer questions about the workplace equipment in 2A.
Use the words in the box.

| check in to work | get a drink of water | read email | make copies | move boxes |
| print documents | lift heavy objects | store files | type email | |

A: What do we use the photocopier for?

B: To make copies of documents.

D Think about it. Ask and answer the questions with your classmates.

1. For what other reasons do we use each piece of equipment?

2. Which equipment do you know how to use?

▶▶ **TEST YOURSELF**

Copy the chart in your notebook. Put words
from the lesson in the chart.

Deductions	Earnings	Equipment

1 Prepare to write

A **Look at the pictures in 1B. Guess the answers.**

1. What does Lucy do?

2. What skills does she need in her job?

B **Look at the pictures. Listen to Lucy's email.**
2-05

C **Listen again and read Lucy's email.**
2-05

Subject: My new job

Hi Emilia,

How are you? How's your family?

I started my new job three weeks ago. I work as a sandwich chef at the deli counter in the supermarket. Work starts at 7 a.m, and I have to get up early to be on time.

The job has a lot of health and safety regulations. We have to keep our hands and tools clean. I have to use plastic gloves to prepare the food. Remember my long hair? It's in a hairnet because it might get into the food.

My co-workers are friendly, and we're a great team. I like to talk to the customers, too. I'm very happy with my new job.

Tell me your news. How do you like your job?

Take care,

Lucy

> **WRITER'S NOTE**
> Use informal greetings in an email to a friend, such as "Hi," or "Hey." Then continue with a friendly question.

D **Check your understanding. Circle *a* or *b*.**

1. Lucy is a _____ .   a. cashier   b. sandwich chef

2. Lucy wears a _____ at work.   a. hat   b. hairnet

3. Lucy works _____ .   a. on a team   b. alone

🔊 **E** **Listen to the conversation. Check (✓) the types of work behavior you hear.**
2-06

✓ Be on time for work.

_____ Listen carefully to instructions.

_____ Check in with your time card in the morning.

_____ Follow safety procedures.

_____ Check off the delivery times on a list.

_____ Wear appropriate clothing.

_____ Ask for help.

_____ Smile when you talk to customers.

🔊 **F** **Compare answers with your partner. Listen again and check your work.**
2-06

2 Plan

A **Think about your job, your English class, or another class. What are some rules? Make a list.**

B **Talk to a partner. Tell your partner about rules and regulations at your workplace or school.**

We have to wear a uniform. We can't chew gum.

NEED HELP?

We can't…
smoke.
listen to music.
make phone calls.

3 Write

A **Write an email. Tell a friend about rules and regulations at your job, in your English class, or in another class.**

○ ○ ○

Subject: _____

Dear _____ ,

    How are you? How's your _____ ? I started my new _____ _____ _____ ago. I like it very much. We have a few rules. We have to _____ and _____ . We can't _____ or _____ . We can _____ , but we can't _____ . These rules are important because _____ . Tell me your news. How is your job? Do you like it?

All the best,

_____

B **Share your email. Read your email to a partner.**

▶▶ **TEST YOURSELF**

Complete the following sentences. Share your responses with your teacher.

1. After this writing lesson, I can…
2. I need more help with…

1 Explore talking about possibility using *might* and *might not*

2-07

A Listen and read the conversation. What are two requests that Hiroko makes? Why?

Hiroko: Martin, there's some water on the floor over here. Can you put up a warning sign, please?

Martin: Yes, of course. I'll put a sign on the floor. Someone might slip and fall.

Hiroko: Thank you, and could you put these cleaning products in the closet?

Martin: Yes, they might be dangerous. And I'll put another sign on the wall. Some people might not notice the sign on the floor.

B Analyze the conversation in 1A. What kind of word follows *might* and *might not*?

C Study the grammar. Read the charts.

Might and *might not*						
Affirmative statements			**Negative statements**			
I You He She We They	might	get hurt. have an accident. start a fire.	I You He She We They	might not	be safe. see the sign.	

D Work with the grammar. Complete the sentences. Use *might* or *might not* and the verbs in the box.

> **GRAMMAR NOTE**
>
> We use *might* to say that something is possible. Do not use *to* after *might*.

break in	fall	get hurt	have	hear	see

1. The warehouse floor is wet. Someone <u>might fall</u> .

2. Joe didn't lock the warehouse's back door. Someone _____ .

3. Alex isn't wearing his hard hat. He _____ .

4. Maria isn't wearing her glasses. She _____ the warning sign.

5. Martin is pushing the hand cart too fast. He _____ an accident.

6. Dan is listening to loud music on his headphones. He _____ the fire alarm.

2 Practice *should* and *should not*

A Study the grammar. Read the charts. Listen to the sentences.

2-08

Should and should not

Affirmative statements			Negative statements		
I You He She We They	should	wear safety gloves. lock the door.	I You He She We They	should not (shouldn't)	touch the fire alarm. use the fire exit.

B Check your understanding. Complete the sentences. Use *should* or *shouldn't*.

1. This road is dangerous. You <u>should</u> drive slowly.

2. There's some smoke in the kitchen. You _____ press the fire alarm.

3. You _____ use this elevator. It's not working.

4. They _____ walk on the wet floor. They might slip.

5. It's going to rain. You _____ take an umbrella.

6. It's sunny today. We _____ wear sunscreen.

> **GRAMMAR NOTE**
>
> Use *should* if you think something is a good idea.
>
> Use *shouldn't* if you think that something is a bad idea, or to give a warning.

3 Practice using *might* and *should*

A Complete the sentences. Use *might (not)*, *should (not)*, and the words in the box.

| breathe in | get burned | fall | get dirty | get injured |

1. You <u>shouldn't</u> go to a construction site without a hard hat.
   Something <u>might fall</u> on your head.

2. You _____ work without a face mask. You _____ the dust.

3. You _____ wear safety glasses. Your eyes _____ .

4. You _____ wear safety gloves. Your hands _____ by hot machines.

5. You _____ work without a uniform. Your clothes _____ .

B Work with a partner. Look at the photos. What might happen? What should each person do?

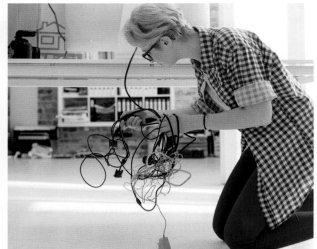

A: *The floor is wet. Someone might fall.*

B: *Yes. He should put up a warning sign.*

C Write two sentences in your notebook about each picture in 3B.

4 Give and respond to advice at work

A Read the problems. Work in a group. What should the people do?

1. My boss always asks us to stay late.
2. I don't have safety equipment at work.
3. My co-workers always ask me to help them.
4. My co-workers don't clean up in the kitchen.
5. I don't understand how to use the safety equipment.

A: *My boss always asks us to stay late.*

B: *You should talk to your boss.*

A: *Yes, but he might get upset…*

B Talk about your answers with your class.

▶▶TEST YOURSELF

Close your book. Write two sentences about things you should do at work or at school. Read your sentences to a partner. Then say what might or might not happen if you don't do these things.

1 Listen to learn: Job instructions

A Look at the pictures. Which of these tasks can you do?

make copies   operate a forklift   mail a package   use power tools   write an email

 2-09 **B** Listen to three conversations. Where are these people?

 2-09 **C** Listen again. Write each person's task under the pictures.

Jung-ju   Ruth   Simon

1. _____   2. _____   3. _____

D Discuss this question with your classmates:

What kind of requests do you sometimes need to make at work?

2 Practice your pronunciation

2-10 **A** Listen to the two versions of the conversation below. In which version does Simon sound more helpful? Check (✔) your answer.

Ruth: Could you help me with my computer, please?

Simon: I'm busy now, but I'll help you later. OK?

☐ Conversation 1
☐ Conversation 2

> **NEED HELP?**
>
> Intonation and word stress can show how a person feels.
> Is she upset?
> Does he want to help?

2-11 **B** Listen to the conversations. Then practice with a partner.

1. **A:** Could you make some photocopies, please?

   B: Yes, of course.

2. **A:** Could you type these letters, please?

   B: Sure! No problem. I can type them this afternoon.

3 Practice making requests with *can* and *could*

<audio>2-12</audio> **A** Listen and read the conversation. Identify one instruction and one request.

Rachel: John, could you make some copies for me, please?

John: Yes, of course. How many do you need?

Rachel: I need fifteen copies.

John: I'll do it right away. Wait a minute—did you say **fifty** or **fifteen** copies?

Rachel: **Fifteen.** Thanks for checking!

John: By the way, could I take my lunch break early today? I need to go to the dentist.

Rachel: That's no problem.

<audio>2-13</audio> **B** Listen and mark the answers to the questions.

1. a. Yes, she did.   b. No, she didn't.   3. a. Yes, he did.   b. No, he didn't.

2. a. Yes, he did.   b. No, he didn't.   4. a. Yes, she did.   b. No, she didn't.

C Think about the grammar. When do we use *can I*? When do we use *can you*?

Making requests		
Can	you	open this box, please?
Could		help me with this computer?
Can	I	use this photocopier?
Could		come in at 8 a.m. tomorrow?
Could is more formal and more polite than *can*. If you are making a big request, it is better to use *could*.		

D Talk to a partner. Take turns making and responding to requests. Give a reason for each request.

1. You need to change your work schedule from Saturday and Sunday to Monday and Tuesday.

2. You want to open the window.

3. You need to ask your boss to sign a letter.

4. You want to borrow your friend's cell phone.

5. You want to go home early today.

A: *Could I work on Monday and Tuesday next week? I have to visit my family on Saturday and Sunday.*

B: *Yes. You can have the weekend off.*

> **NEED HELP?**
>
> Respond to requests.
> Yes, of course.
> Yes, that's fine.
> No problem.
> Sure!
> Just a minute.
> Sorry, that's not possible.

4 Make conversation: clarify instructions and make requests

A Work with a partner. Make new conversations.
Use the situations in the boxes.

A: _____ , could you _____ , please?

B: Yes, of course. _____ ?

A: _____ .

B: I'll do it right away. Did you say _____ or _____ ?

A: _____ . Thanks for checking.

B: By the way, could I _____ ? I have to _____ .

A: That's no problem.

| deliver this to room 115/150 |
| call Mr. Jones/Mr. Johnson |
| schedule a meeting on May 13/14 |

| go home early |
| come in late |
| take a vacation day |

B Present your conversation to another pair. Observe their conversation.

AT WORK ▶ Requesting a schedule change

A Listen to different ways to request a schedule change.

2-14

A: Could I come in on Tuesday instead of Monday? There's an event at my son's school.

B: OK.

A: Could I work at night next week? I have to take care of my mom during the day.

B: Sure. That's fine.

A: Could I switch my schedule? I want to take a computer class at the college.

B: Yes, I think that's OK.

B Talk to a partner. Practice the conversations in A.

C Think about it. Ask and answer the questions with your classmates.

1. What kinds of reasons do the people in A give for their requests?

2. When do you think it's OK to ask for a schedule change? When is it not OK?

▶▶ TEST YOURSELF

Act out this situation with a classmate. Take turns with each role.

Employee: Ask for a schedule change at work.
Manager: Respond to your employee's request.

1 Build reading strategies

A Circle the correct words to complete the definitions. Check your answers in a dictionary.

positive attitude: a (cheerful / sad) way to think or feel about a situation

complain: say that you are (happy / unhappy) with something

cooperate: work (well / badly) with other people

get a promotion: get a (better / worse) job at the same company

B Read the title of the article below. What do you think? Which words describe a positive attitude at work? Circle them.

| angry | excited | friendly | worried | bored |

> **READER'S NOTE**
> Identify reasons. Which paragraph tells you *why* you should have a positive attitude? How many reasons are there?

C Read the article. When can you use this advice?

A Positive Attitude

When you start a new job, it's important to show that you have a positive attitude.

Show that you want to learn. Read and listen to instructions carefully. Be sure you know the rules of the company. Ask questions. It's okay to make mistakes, but you should show that you want to improve[1]. Ask your manager for new tasks. This will help with your performance evaluation[2].

Show that you can cooperate. Don't just complain about problems. Look for solutions. Look for ways to help co-workers. Answer questions and speak to your co-workers in a helpful way. Ask them for feedback[3] on how you are working.

As Penny Loretto of *The Balance* says, supervisors and co-workers value people with a positive attitude, and it also makes your job more pleasant and fun. It can help you keep your job and get a promotion too.

[1] improve: make something better
[2] performance evaluation: job report from your manager
[3] feedback: their opinion of your work

Source: *thebalance.com*

 D Listen and read the article again. Which of these things do you do in your job or at school?
2-15

E **Choose the correct words. Fill in the bubble next to the correct answer.**

1. You don't understand the instructions.
   You should _____ .
   - ⓐ make mistakes
   - ⓑ change your job
   - ⓒ ask questions

2. You want to show that you can cooperate.
   You should _____ .
   - ⓐ work alone
   - ⓑ help your co-workers
   - ⓒ complain

3. You find a problem at work.
   You should _____ .
   - ⓐ complain
   - ⓑ say nothing
   - ⓒ suggest a solution

4. According to the article, a positive attitude can _____ .
   - ⓐ make your job fun
   - ⓑ improve your listening skills
   - ⓒ answer questions

F **Complete the sentences. Use the words in the box.**

attitude	improve	cooperate	complain

1. When you work with other people, it's important to _____ .
2. Some employees _____ a lot about problems. This shows a negative attitude.
3. He has a positive _____ . He is always cheerful and helpful.
4. A good employee tries to _____ his or her performance evaluation every year.

2 Interpret a performance evaluation

A **Read Rosa's performance evaluation. What are the problems in her evaluation?**

Employee name: Rosa Pereira	COMMENTS:
Follows instructions:	She asks good questions.
Helps others:	She explains instructions to her coworkers.
Uses time:	Sometimes she talks too much and doesn't finish her work.
Solves problems:	She made a new sign with instructions for the photocopier.
Shows a positive attitude:	She is polite and friendly. She talks to customers.
Is on time for work:	She was late for work three times in March.
Evaluation score: Excellent Good Fair	**Signature:** Max Rossi (Manager)

B **Think about it. Discuss these questions with your classmates: How should the manager evaluate Rosa? Why? Are performance evaluations a good idea? Why?**

 BRING IT TO LIFE

For one week, record examples of co-workers', classmates', and friends' positive attitudes, problem solving, and cooperation. Tell the class about them.

TEAMWORK & LANGUAGE REVIEW

A **Look at the picture. Ask and answer the questions with your classmates.**

1. How many jobs can you name?
2. Choose one person in the picture. What skills does this person need for his or her job?
3. What is one skill you need in all of these jobs?
4. Look at the two men in red. What are they saying?
5. Would you like to work in a hotel? Why or why not?

B **With your group, write six requests that people in the picture might make.**

Could you park my car, please?

C **With your group, write eight pieces of advice for people in this workplace.**

You should greet hotel guests with a smile.

D **Work with a partner. Complete the conversation with *could*, *should*, or *might*. Then practice the conversation.**

A: _____ you take this luggage upstairs, please?

B: Yes, of course. What's the room number?

A: It's room 238. You _____ use the rear elevator. The front elevator _____ be busy.

B: Did you say 238 or 258?

A: 238.

B: OK. And _____ I switch my schedule tomorrow? I need to go to the doctor in the morning. _____ I start work at 10 a.m.?

A: Yes, that's fine, but you _____ need to work later in the afternoon.

B: That's no problem. Thank you.

E Read Ellen's to-do list. Work with a partner to decide the best sequence for the tasks.

A: *I think Ellen should finish the report first because she needs it for the meeting.*

B: *Well, I think she should make a dental appointment. Her health is very important.*

Task	Importance
Prepare for meeting about the report	
Review notes about last week's meeting	
Finish report	
Send an email to customers	
Make a dental appointment	

F Help your partner make a to-do list for your week.

Task	Importance	Due date

G Share your lists with your group. Analyze the to-do lists. What types of tasks are the same for everyone? Which tasks are different? What advice do you have for each other?

PROBLEM SOLVING AT WORK

A Listen and read about Jamal.

2-16

> Jamal started a new job. He works as a ticket collector in the movie theater. He is on time every day. He wears neat clothes. He's a good worker, but he is sometimes nervous. He doesn't always understand the manager's instructions. Once he didn't go to work because he didn't understand a schedule change. He doesn't like to ask questions about the instructions, and sometimes he makes mistakes.

B Work with your classmates. Answer the questions.

1. What is Jamal's problem?
2. Why do you think he doesn't like to ask questions?
3. What should he do? Think of two or three solutions to his problem.

UNIT

6 On the Phone

A LOOK AT
- Phone bills and using phones
- Present continuous and simple present
- Apologizing and making excuses

LESSON 1 VOCABULARY

1 Learn about phone bills

A Show what you know. Circle the words you know.

1. billing period
2. previous charges
3. total due
4. monthly charges
5. data allowance
6. carrier

B Listen and look at the phone bill. What different kinds of charges are there?

2-17

PERFECT PHONE PP 6

Talk and text anywhere with your Perfect Phone!

BILL SUMMARY

For 401-555-2615

1. From 07/22/17 to 08/21/17
2. Previous Balance $78.75
   Payment received 08/03/17
   Thank you!
3. TOTAL DUE **$86.60**
   Due 09/18/2017

PERFECT PHONE PP

PLANS AND SERVICES
Service for July 22–August 21 $50.00
Unlimited messaging included
Data charges (4 GB) $25.00
4. Total monthly charges $75.00

PERFECT PHONE PP

5. **Data usage summary**
   Used 3.9 GB
   Allowance 4 GB

Messaging summary
Text messages incoming 1652
Text messages outgoing 1097

Voice usage summary
Mobile to mobile (unlimited) 500 minute
Nights and weekends (unlimited) 347 minute

C Listen and repeat the words from 1A.

2-18

D Write the vocabulary. Look at the phone bill. Complete the sentences.

1. The <u>previous charges</u> on Walter's phone bill were $78.75.
2. Walter pays $75.00 for his _____ .
3. He watched a lot of videos and used most of his _____ .
4. The name of his _____ is Perfect Phone.
5. The _____ is from July 22 to August 21.
6. The _____ for this billing period is $86.60.

NEED HELP?

You use data when you check email, use the Internet, and watch videos.

E Ask and answer these questions with your partner.

1. What do you mainly use your phone for: voice calls, texting, or data?
2. What kind of phone plan do you have?
3. How many phone calls or text messages do you make or send a day? A week?
4. What additional charges are there on your phone bill?

2 Talk about using phones

A Work with your classmates. Match the words with the pictures.

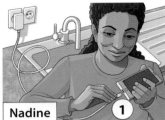

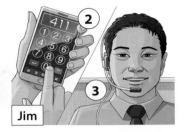

__1__	phone charger	_____	make an emergency call
_____	headset	_____	send a text message
_____	listen to voice mail	_____	leave a message
_____	call directory assistance	_____	use an app

2-19

B Listen and check your answers. Then talk to a partner about the pictures in 2A.

A: *What is Nadine doing?*

B: *She's using her phone charger.*

C Think about it. Ask and answer the questions with your classmates.

1. Do you use a home phone, a cell phone, or a computer for phone calls? Which do you prefer? Why?

2. Where do you store the phone numbers for calls you make regularly: in your head, on your phone, or in a phone book?

▶▶ **TEST YOURSELF**

Copy the chart in your notebook. Put words from the lesson into the chart.

Phone charges	Phone equipment	Types of communication

1 Prepare to write

A Look at the pictures. Match the sentences with the pictures.

I called my son's school. _____

I wrote an absence note. _____

I was worried. _____

B Listen and read Jennifer's story.

2-20

Calling in Sick

Yesterday morning, my son Joshua overslept. He never oversleeps. He usually gets up before me! He had a fever and a sore throat. I was very worried.

First, I called the doctor. He said Joshua should stay in bed. Then I called my office. They don't like it when employees call in sick, but I can work more hours this weekend. After that, I called Joshua's school to report his absence.

Today, I wrote a note to his teacher to give an excuse for his absence yesterday. Here's what I wrote:

To: bhenson@school.org
From: jsoriano@homeemail.com
Subject: Josh's absence
Dear Mrs. Henson,
    Please excuse Joshua Soriano's absence on October 13. He had a fever and a sore throat. He will return to school today.
Sincerely,
Mrs. Jennifer Soriano

WRITER'S NOTE

In a formal note, start with *Dear Mr.*, *Mrs.*, or *Ms.* and the last name of the person you are writing to. Finish with *Sincerely*, or *Sincerely yours*, and your name.

C Check your understanding. Mark the sentences *T* (true) or *F* (false).

_____ 1. Joshua often oversleeps.

_____ 2. Joshua overslept yesterday.

_____ 3. Jennifer wasn't worried.

_____ 4. Jennifer wrote a note to her job.

_____ 5. Jennifer called in sick.

_____ 6. Jennifer can't work more hours this weekend.

D Listen to the call. Circle the answers.

2-21

1. Who is calling?   a. Central Electric   b. Jennifer
2. Who is she calling?   a. Jennifer   b. Kelly Donaldson
3. Why is she calling?   a. Her son is sick.   b. She needs information.

E Compare answers with your partner. Listen again and check your work.

2-21

2 Plan

A Think of a time when you called in sick to work or to school, for yourself or for a child. Copy the chart into your notebook. Complete the chart with details about your experience.

1. When did you call in sick? What was the problem?
2. What steps did you take? What did you do first, second, and third?
3. What did you do in the end? Did you write an email or a note to the teacher? Did you write an email or talk with your employer?

1		
2 Step 1	Step 2	Step 3
3		

B Talk to your partner about your chart. Ask questions to help your partner add more details to their chart.

3 Write

A Write a description of your experience. Then write a short email or note to explain your absence.

_____ , I _____ . I had a _____ and a _____ . First, I _____ . He/She said _____ . Then I _____ . The next day, I wrote a _____ to _____ . Here's what I wrote:

```
○ ○ ○

Dear _____ ,
Please excuse _____ absence on _____ .
_____ was _____ . _____ will return to
_____ on _____ .
_____ ,
_____
```

B Read your note to a partner. Say something you like about your partner's note.

▶▶ TEST YOURSELF

Complete the following sentences. Share your responses with your teacher.

1. After this writing lesson, I can…
2. I need more help with…

1 Contrast the present continuous and simple present

A Look at the pictures. Listen. What are they doing?

2-22

James: Hi. Do you have a minute?

Tania: Not really. I'm jogging right now.

James: At 6 a.m.?

Tania: Yes. I usually jog from 6:00 to 6:30 every morning.

Kyra: Hi. Do you have time to talk?

Stan: Sorry, I can't. We're eating dinner right now.

Kyra: Dinner at 4 p.m.?

Stan: Uh-huh. We always eat early on Fridays. We go to a dance class at 6:00.

B Analyze the conversations in 1A. Which verbs describe something you do regularly? Which verbs describe something you are doing now?

C Study the grammar. Read the chart. When do we use the verbs *be* and *do*?

The present continuous and the simple present						
Simple present affirmative and negative statements						
I	work		We			
You	don't work	every day.	You	work	every day.	
He	works			don't work		
She	doesn't work		They			

GRAMMAR NOTE

Use the simple present to talk about activities you do every day (routines). Use the present continuous to talk about activities that are happening now.

Present continuous affirmative and negative statements						
I	am am/'m not		We			
You	are aren't	working	right now.	You	are aren't	working	right now.
He She	is isn't		They			

D Work with a partner. Make sentences about Tania and Stan. Use the information in 1A and your own ideas.

2 Practice: information questions in the present

🔊 2-23 **A** Study the grammar. Read the chart. Listen to the conversations.

Information questions and answers	
A: How often do you talk on the phone? **B:** I talk on the phone every day.	**A:** What are you doing now? **B:** I'm texting my friend.
A: When does she usually get home? **B:** She usually gets home at 6:00.	**A:** What is she studying right now? **B:** She's studying science.

SPELLING NOTE

Verbs with -ing

For words that end in -e, change the -e to -ing.
live → living

B Check your understanding. Complete the information questions.

1. How often _do they talk_ on the phone? (they, talk)

2. What _____ about right now? (you, talk)

3. What time _____ every day? (she, get up)

4. What _____ today? (we, study)

5. Where _____ at the moment? (he, live)

6. How many hours _____ every night? (she, sleep)

3 Practice: *Yes/no* questions in the present

🔊 2-24 **A** Study the grammar. Read the chart. Listen to the conversations.

Yes/no questions and answers	
A: Does she call you every day? **B:** Yes, she does.	**A:** Are you eating dinner right now? **B:** Yes, I am.
A: Do they talk on the phone every day? **B:** No, they don't.	**A:** Is she watching TV at the moment? **B:** No, she isn't.

B Look at the pictures in 1A. Complete the questions. Then write the answers.

1. _____ on the phone right now? (she, talk)

   _____

2. _____ at the gym right now? (she, exercise)

   _____

3. _____ dinner now? (they, eat)

   _____

4. _____ a movie now? (they, watch)

   _____

4 Ask and answer questions in the present

A Look at the pictures. Ask questions about what the people do every day and what they are doing now.

A: *What does he do?*

B: *He makes furniture.*

A: *Is he using a saw right now?*

B: *Yes, he is.*

B Listen to the conversations. Complete the chart about what these people are doing now and what they usually do.

2-25

	Barry	Cindy	Andrew	Lianne
now				
usually				

C Talk with a partner. Ask and answer questions about the four people in 4B.

D Work with a team. Make five questions with simple present or present continuous verbs. Then ask your classmates.

Do you read a newspaper every day?

Are you wearing something new today?

E Write four sentences about the answers from 4D. Then share your answers with the class.

Fernando reads a newspaper every day.

Elena is wearing a new jacket today.

▶▶ TEST YOURSELF

Describe a friend. What does he or she do every day? What is he or she doing right now? Write four sentences.

1 Listen to learn: leaving and taking messages

A **Read the telephone message. Answer the questions.**

1. Who is the message from?

2. Who is the message for?

3. Is Rita late or out sick? Why?

☎ **IMPORTANT MESSAGE**

from	Rita Gonzalez
for	Ms. Mendoza
message	Rita is out sick today.
	She has a bad cold.

B **Listen to the phone calls. Complete the messages.**
2-26

①
For: _____
From: _____
Message: _____
_____

②
For: _____
From: _____
Message: _____
_____

③
For: _____
From: _____
Message: _____
_____

C **Listen again. Complete the phrases.**
2-26

Asking for someone: Can I _____ to Mr. Jackson, please?

Is Mrs. Andrews _____ ?

Leaving a message: Can you _____ her a message?

Can I _____ a message for Mr. Green, please?

Taking a message: Can I _____ a message?

I'll _____ him your message.

2 Practice your pronunciation

A **Listen to the pronunciation of the words.**
2-27

live—I live in California.   leave—I leave work at 5:00.

B **Listen. Circle the words you hear.**
2-28

1. live   leave   2. his   he's   3. fill   feel   4. will   we'll

C **Listen and repeat.**
2-29

1. I don't feel well.   3. Can I leave a message?

2. He's calling in sick.   4. I will pay my phone bill.

D **Talk to a partner. Take turns reading the sentences in 2C. Ask for feedback.**

3 Practice using indirect objects

A Listen and read the conversation. What will Fiona give? Who will she give it to?

2-30

Jack: Hello. Can I speak to Mr. Reed, please?

Fiona: He's not here right now. Can I take a message?

Jack: This is Jack Brown. I'm the new office assistant. I can't come in today.

Fiona: Oh, what's the problem?

Jack: I have a bad cold. I have to go to the doctor.

Fiona: I'm sorry to hear that.

Jack: I'll be back to work tomorrow.

Fiona: OK. I'll give him your message. Thanks for calling.

Jack: Thank you. Goodbye.

B Listen and mark the answers to the questions.

2-31

1. a. Yes, he is.   b. No, he isn't.   3. a. Yes, he does.   b. No, he doesn't.
2. a. Yes, he is.   b. No, he isn't.   4. a. Yes, he will.   b. No, he won't.

C Think about the grammar. Look at the conversation.

1. Identify a sentence using the verb *give*.
2. This verb has two objects. Which is a direct object and which is an indirect object?

D Study the grammar.

Verbs with direct and indirect objects		
	direct object	**indirect object**
I'll give	the message	to him.
	indirect object	**direct object**
I'll give	him	the message.
Some verbs, such as *give*, *send*, *show*, and *write*, can have two objects. When the indirect object follows the direct object, we use the prepositions *to* or *for*.		

E Talk to a partner. Make questions and answers using the words provided.

A: *Can you give the message to him?*

B: *Yes, I'll give him the message.*

1. give a message / him   4. show your photos / me / you
2. send an email / her   5. give a call / us / you
3. write a letter / them

4 Make conversation: leaving a message and making an excuse

A Work with a partner. Make a new conversation.

> A: Hello. May I speak to _____ , please?
>
> B: He's not here right now. Can I take a message?
>
> A: This is _____ . I'm _____ . I'm going to be _____ today.
>
> B: Oh, what's the problem?
>
> A: I have _____ . I have to _____ .
>
> B: _____ .
>
> A: I'll be back to work _____ .
>
> B: I'll give _____ the message. Thanks for calling.
>
> A: Thank you. Goodbye.

NEED HELP?

Express concern:
I'm sorry to hear that!
That's too bad!
I hope you feel better soon.
Take care!

B Present your conversation to another pair. Observe their conversation.

AT WORK Apologizing and making an excuse

A Listen and read the conversations. Identify two ways to make an apology and two excuses.

> A: Sorry I'm late. My flight was delayed.
>
> B: That's OK. Please come and sit down.

> A: I apologize for mixing up the orders. It was a mistake.
>
> B: Make sure it doesn't happen again.

B Work with a partner. Practice the conversations in A. Continue the conversations using your own ideas.

C Tell a partner about something you apologized for at work or at school recently.

▶▶ TEST YOURSELF

Act out this situation with a classmate. Take turns with each role.

Construction worker: Apologize for a mistake on the job. Give an excuse.
Supervisor: Respond to the apology and accept the excuse.

1 **Build reading strategies**

A Read the definitions. Which words describe the people in the picture? What do you think they are doing?

counselor: someone who gives you advice

senior: an older person, often a retired person

volunteer: someone who works to help others and isn't paid

B Underline the root word in *counselor*. What other job names end in *-or*?

C Preview the web page below. Scan the headings. Which of these places are asking for volunteers, and which are offering help?

D Read the web page. Which groups give advice?

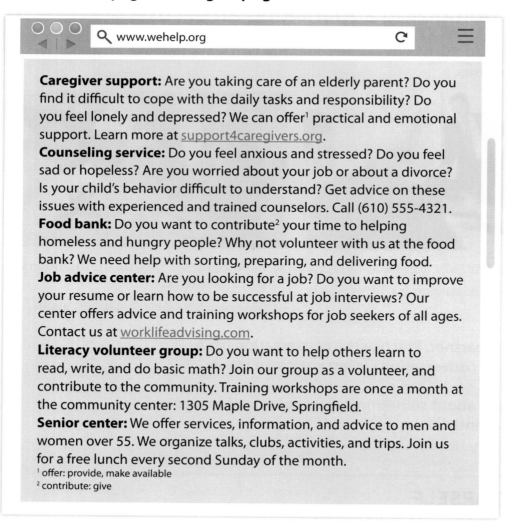

www.wehelp.org

Caregiver support: Are you taking care of an elderly parent? Do you find it difficult to cope with the daily tasks and responsibility? Do you feel lonely and depressed? We can offer[1] practical and emotional support. Learn more at support4caregivers.org.

Counseling service: Do you feel anxious and stressed? Do you feel sad or hopeless? Are you worried about your job or about a divorce? Is your child's behavior difficult to understand? Get advice on these issues with experienced and trained counselors. Call (610) 555-4321.

Food bank: Do you want to contribute[2] your time to helping homeless and hungry people? Why not volunteer with us at the food bank? We need help with sorting, preparing, and delivering food.

Job advice center: Are you looking for a job? Do you want to improve your resume or learn how to be successful at job interviews? Our center offers advice and training workshops for job seekers of all ages. Contact us at worklifeadvising.com.

Literacy volunteer group: Do you want to help others learn to read, write, and do basic math? Join our group as a volunteer, and contribute to the community. Training workshops are once a month at the community center: 1305 Maple Drive, Springfield.

Senior center: We offer services, information, and advice to men and women over 55. We organize talks, clubs, activities, and trips. Join us for a free lunch every second Sunday of the month.

[1] offer: provide, make available
[2] contribute: give

READER'S NOTE

Links that end in .com are private organizations that usually charge money for their services. Links that end in .org are usually non-profit organizations.

2-33

E Listen and read the web page again. Which organizations are you interested in?

F **Read the questions. Fill in the bubble next to the correct answer.**

1. What is the best title for this page?
   - ⓐ Community Services
   - ⓑ Medical Help Centers
   - ⓒ Educational Opportunities

2. My grandmother wants to make some friends. Where should she go?
   - ⓐ Caregiver support
   - ⓑ Literacy volunteer group
   - ⓒ Senior center

3. I want to help teach other people. Where should I go?
   - ⓐ Job advice center
   - ⓑ Food bank
   - ⓒ Literacy volunteer group

4. Which of these probably charges money for their services?
   - ⓐ Literacy volunteer group
   - ⓑ Job advice center
   - ⓒ Food bank

G **Complete the sentences. Use the words in the box.**

| offer | contribute | senior | volunteer |

1. A place where older people can meet is a _____ center.
2. You can _____ to your community by helping others.
3. Some people _____ to help prepare meals for the homeless.
4. Public libraries usually _____ free Internet service.

2 Read a bar chart about volunteering

A **Look at the bar chart. Then answer the questions.**

1. What do the colors red and blue represent?
2. What do the six sets of bars represent?
3. What does the chart tell us about women volunteers?
4. What does the chart tell us about senior volunteers?

B **Think about it. Talk about these questions with your classmates.**

1. What kind of volunteer activities interest you?
2. What do you think are the advantages of volunteering?

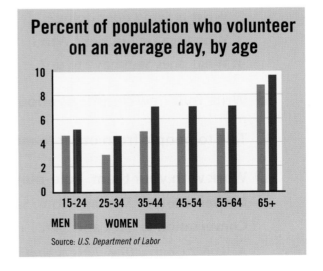

Percent of population who volunteer on an average day, by age

MEN WOMEN

Source: *U.S. Department of Labor*

🔘 BRING IT TO LIFE

Find the names, addresses, and phone numbers of three community services in your neighborhood on the Internet. Make a list of the services with your classmates.

A **Work with a team. Look at the picture. Answer the questions.**

1. What do you see in the picture?
2. What is Sam Lopez doing?
3. Who is calling in sick? Why?
4. What does Sam have to do?

B **Write four new questions about the picture.**

C **Talk to people from other teams. Ask your questions.**

D **Work with your team. Role-play two conversations of 6–8 lines each.**

Conversation 1: Sam and Tom; Sam is calling in sick.

Conversation 2: Jack and Sam's assistant, Jessica; Jack is leaving a message for Sam.

A: *Lopez Contracting. This is Sam Lopez.*

B: *Sam. It's Tom.*

A: *Hi, Tom. Where are you?*

B: *…*

E **Work with your class. Write a paragraph about the picture.**

Today is a bad day for Sam Lopez…

F Work in a team. Make a list of all the different things you regularly do with your phone. Categorize them and write them in the chart. Use the ideas in the box and your own ideas.

use a GPS app	take photos	take videos	play games
send texts	get a taxi	order take-out food	read email

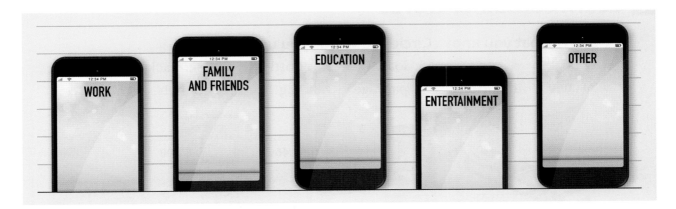

G Individually, choose one of the topics below. Complete the sentence with your ideas. Then share your ideas with your team.

1. It's very useful to have a phone when _____

   _____

2. It makes me upset when people use their phones _____

   _____

3. It's dangerous to use your phone when _____

   _____

PROBLEM SOLVING AT WORK

2-34

A Listen and read about Janet.

> Janet's son, Timmy, is three years old. She takes him to a childcare center every morning at 7:00. Then she goes to work. Timmy often gets sick. Last winter he had colds four different times. Timmy is sick again today, and he can't go to the childcare center. Janet can't stay home with him. She has to go to work. She has no more sick days this year.

B Work with your classmates. Answer the questions.

1. What is Janet's problem?
2. What can she do? Think of two or three solutions to her problem.

What's for Dinner?

A LOOK AT
- Food containers and measurements
- Count and noncount nouns
- Offering and asking for help

LESSON 1 VOCABULARY

1 Learn container words

A Show what you know. Circle the words you use.

1. box
2. jar
3. can
4. carton
5. loaf
6. package
7. bottle
8. bag
9. six-pack
10. bunch

B Listen and look at the pictures. Which words are not container words?
2-35

C Listen and repeat the words from 1A.
2-36

D Write the vocabulary. Look at the pictures. Complete the sentences.

1. A _carton_ of milk is $2.08.
2. A _____ of oil is $6.09.
3. A _____ of peanut butter is $3.40.
4. A _____ of potato chips is $1.99.
5. A _____ of bread is $2.49.
6. A _____ of bananas is $1.59.
7. A _____ of soup is $1.46.
8. A _____ of spaghetti is $1.49.
9. A _____ of cookies is $2.99.
10. A _____ of soda is $3.59.

E Talk to a partner. Ask and answer the questions.

Which of these food items do you buy regularly?
How much do they cost?

2 Talk about weights and measurements

A Work in a team. Match the words with the picture.

Conversions

1 gallon (gal.) = 4 quarts
1 quart (qt.) = 2 pints
1 pint (pt.) = 2 cups
1 cup (c.) = 8 ounces (oz.)
1 pound (lb.) = 16 ounces
1 tablespoon (tbsp.) = 3 teaspoons (tsp.)

_____ one cup of flour

_____ one gallon of water

_____ one pint of milk

_____ one quart of milk

_____ one tablespoon of sugar

_____ one teaspoon of salt

_____ twelve ounces of oil

__1__ two pounds of flour

B Listen and check your answers. Then practice the words with a partner.

2-37

C Complete the sentences. Use the list of equivalents in 2A.

1. There are 16 _ounces_ in 1 pound of flour.

2. There are 2 _____ in 1 quart of milk.

3. There are 4 quarts in 1 _____ of water.

4. There are 3 _____ in 1 tablespoon of sugar.

5. There are 8 _____ in 1 cup of milk.

D Think about it. Ask and answer the questions with your classmates.

1. Which foods do you usually measure? Which weights and measurements do you use? When?

2. Look at the containers in 1A. How much is usually in each type of container? What are the containers made from?

▸▸ **TEST YOURSELF**

Copy the chart in your notebook. Put the container words and measurement words from the lesson in the chart.

	milk, water	flour, sugar	oranges, apples	cookies, cereal
Container				
Measurement				

1 Prepare to write

A Look at the pictures. Which words do you know? Where can you find these items?

🔊 **B** Look at the pictures. Listen to the blog post.
2-38

supermarket flyer

coupon

store brand

UNIT PRICE
28¢ per oz.
you pay
$1.68
6 oz.

unit-price label

$1.29

$1.00 OFF

🔊 **C** Listen again and read the blog post.
2-38

Photos (51)

Notes

Friends

Save Money at the Supermarket

Posted by Jung Kim

It's important for me to save money at the supermarket. I have five children, and they eat a lot! I go to the supermarket once a week. Before I go, I read the supermarket flyers and compare prices at different stores. Then I look for coupons in the newspaper and on the Internet. At the supermarket, I check the unit prices and compare different brands. I often buy the store brands. They're usually cheaper than name brands. When I'm ready to pay, I take out all my coupons and give them to the cashier. I bring my own bags to the supermarket because my supermarket charges for plastic bags, and it is good for the environment!

> **WRITER'S NOTE**
> Writers use a *topic sentence*, usually at the beginning of the paragraph, to introduce the main topic.

D Check your understanding. Mark the sentences *T* (true) or *F* (false).

_____ 1. Jung Kim goes to the supermarket every day.

_____ 2. She compares prices in different stores.

_____ 3. She looks for coupons on the Internet.

_____ 4. She often forgets her coupons when she's ready to pay.

_____ 5. She brings her own bags because it saves money.

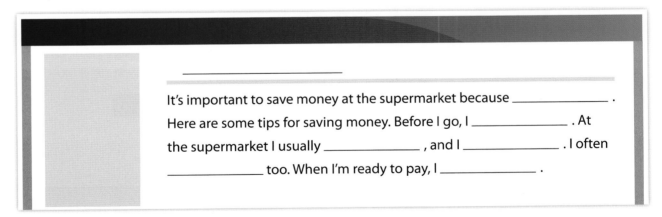

E Listen to Mrs. Kim and her friend talk about ways to save money. Check (✓) the tips they mention.

2-39

_____ Get the special offers.   _____ Buy store brands.

_____ Compare prices.   _____ Buy larger quantities.

_____ Use a rewards card.   _____ Use coupons.

F Listen again. Write how much Mrs. Kim spends on these food items.

2-39

two jars of jam _____   one container of yogurt _____   ten pounds of rice _____

2 Plan

A Make a list of the ways you save money at the supermarket.

B Read your list to a partner. Then talk about the ways you save money.

> — look at supermarket flyers
> — use coupons
> — only buy food on my shopping list

3 Write

A Write a blog post about the ways you save money at the supermarket. Use your ideas from 2B. Give your post a title.

_____

It's important to save money at the supermarket because _____ .
Here are some tips for saving money. Before I go, I _____ . At
the supermarket I usually _____ , and I _____ . I often
_____ too. When I'm ready to pay, I _____ .

B Share your blog post with a partner. Report one way your partner likes to save money at the market.

▶▶ TEST YOURSELF

Complete the following sentences. Share your responses with your teacher.

1. After this writing lesson, I can…
2. I need more help with…

1 Explore count and noncount nouns

A Listen and read Soledad's favorite recipe. Answer the questions.
2-40

1. How many onions does Soledad need?
2. How much cheese does she need?
3. Is there any sugar in the casserole?

Vegetable Casserole

2 onions	2 tbsp. flour
6 potatoes	8 oz. cheese
6 large mushrooms	1/4 c. milk
4 medium tomatoes	1 tsp. salt
3 tbsp. olive oil	1/2 tsp. pepper

First, chop the onions and the potatoes. Then add the oil to a frying pan and →

B Analyze the recipe in 1A. Complete the chart with the recipe ingredients. How are the noncount nouns different from the count nouns?

Count nouns		Noncount nouns
Singular	Plural	
vegetable	vegetables	olive oil

C Study the grammar. Read the chart.

	Count nouns	Noncount nouns
a, an, or *some*	We need an onion. We need some onions.	We need some flour.
not (+ any)	We don't have any onions. We don't have onions.	We don't have any flour. We don't have flour.

D Read the grammar rules. Mark the sentences T (true) or F (false). Change the false sentences. Make them true.

_____ 1. We use *a* or *an* with noncount nouns.

_____ 2. We use *any* with count nouns.

_____ 3. We use *some* with singular nouns.

_____ 4. We use *a* or *an* with plural nouns.

_____ 5. We use *some* with noncount nouns.

E Complete the sentences. Use *a, an, some,* or *any.*

Five friends need ___some___ food for a party. Nasrin needs _____ ounce of
1   2

chocolate for her cake recipe. Miguel is cooking _____ potatoes for his soup. Lucas
3

is bringing _____ bottle of soda. Vera wants to buy _____ quart of chocolate
4   5

ice cream. She never has _____ ice cream in her freezer. And Amy is buying
6

_____ small pizza for herself. She doesn't want _____ cheese on her pizza!
7   8

2 Practice: questions with *How many* and *How much*

A Study the grammar. What is the answer to each question?

	Count nouns	**Noncount nouns**
How many/much	**How many** mushrooms do we need?	**How much** flour do we need?

B Check your understanding. Circle *a* or *b*.

1. How _____ tomatoes do you need?
   a. many   b. much

2. How _____ milk do we have?
   a. many   b. much

3. How _____ potatoes do I need?
   a. many   b. much

4. How _____ cheese do you have?
   a. many   b. much

C Talk to a partner. Ask and answer questions about the recipe in 1A.
Use *how much* and *how many.*

3 Practice: talking about quantities

A Listen to the chef talk about the items she needs in the restaurant kitchen.
2-41   Complete the list.

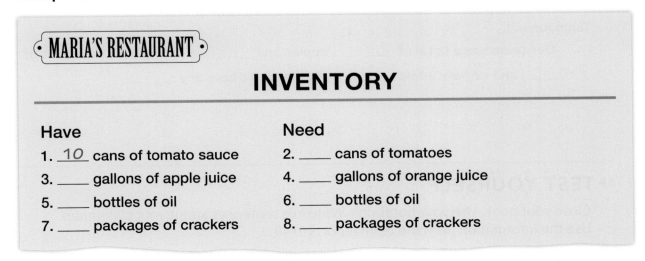

· MARIA'S RESTAURANT ·

INVENTORY

Have
1. _10_ cans of tomato sauce
3. ____ gallons of apple juice
5. ____ bottles of oil
7. ____ packages of crackers

Need
2. ____ cans of tomatoes
4. ____ gallons of orange juice
6. ____ bottles of oil
8. ____ packages of crackers

B Compare answers with a partner. Ask and answer questions about the inventory in 1A.

   A: *How many cans of tomatoes does he have?*

   B: *He doesn't have any cans of tomatoes.*

C In your notebook, make a list of the ingredients for one of your favorite recipes. Dictate the ingredients to your partner. Your partner will ask *How much*? or *How many*? for each ingredient. Then switch roles.

   A: *Flour, F-L-O-U-R.*

   B: *OK, flour. How much flour do I need?*

   A: *You need four cups of flour.*

My partner's recipe for _____

Ingredients	Quantity
_____	_____
_____	_____
_____	_____
_____	_____

4 Ask and answer questions with *How much* and *How many*

A Work with a team. Complete the questions with *How much* or *How many*. Write one more question. Survey your teammates and write their answers in the chart.

Questions	Team members		
1. _____ apples are in your kitchen?			
2. _____ milk is in your refrigerator?			
3. _____ cereal is in your cabinet?			
4. _____ carrots are in your kitchen?			
5. _____ ice cream is in your freezer?			
6. _____ bags of rice are in your cabinet?			
7.			

B Complete the report below with the information from your team. Report your survey results to the class. Work with your class to summarize the class's survey results.

Team Report

   Our team has a total of _____ apples and _____ carrots. We have a lot of

_____ , and we have some _____ , but we don't have any _____ .

▶▶ TEST YOURSELF

Close your book. Use your notebook. Write five sentences about your classmates. Use the information from the team reports in 4B.

Marsha has a gallon of milk in her refrigerator.

1 Listen to learn about the parts of a supermarket

A Look at the pictures. Where can you find these foods?
Write the aisle or section under each food.

grapes _produce_   soup _____

yogurt _____   sausages _____

B Listen to the conversation. Who are the people? What are their jobs?

2-42

C Listen again. Write the aisle number next to each section.
Then write one product you can find in each section.

2-42

Sections	Aisles	Products
Frozen food		
Canned food		
Beverages		
Dairy		

D Discuss this question with your classmates:

What are some other sections of a supermarket? Make a list.

2 Practice your pronunciation

A Listen to the singular and plural forms of these
words. How many syllables are there in each word?

2-43

1. egg   eggs   3. box   boxes

2. apple   apples   4. package   packages

NEED HELP?

Some words end in sounds like *s* (as
in *box* or *dress*), *ge* (as in *page*), or *ch*
(as in *lunch*).

For these words, add an extra
syllable in the plural.

box → boxes

dress → dresses

page → pages

lunch → lunches

B Which plurals have an extra syllable? Write the words in the chart. Then listen
and check your answers. Practice the words with a partner.

2-44

No extra syllable	Extra syllable
grapes	

~~grapes~~	oranges
sausages	lunches
jars	bunches
mushrooms	cartons

3 Review *There is/There are*

 A Listen and read the conversation. Underline two ways to identify
the location of store products.

2-45

Clerk: May I help you?

Customer: Yes, please. Where's the bread?

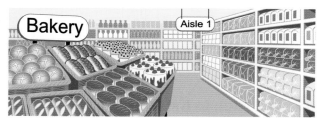

Clerk: There is fresh bread in the bakery section, next to the cakes. Sliced bread is in aisle 1.

Clerk: Do you need anything else?

Customer: Yes. Where are the tomatoes?

Clerk: They're in the produce section, next to the lettuce. There are also canned tomatoes on the top shelf in aisle 2.

 B Listen to the statements. Circle *True* or *False*.

2-46

1. True   False   3. True   False
2. True   False   4. True   False

C Think about the grammar. Look at the conversation and answer the questions.

1. Which form of *be* do you use with noncount nouns?

2. Which form of *be* do you use with singular count nouns?
   With plural count nouns?

4 Make conversation: offer help

A Work with a partner. Make a new conversation.
Use the shopping list or your own ideas.

A: _____ ?

B: I'm looking for some _____ . Which aisle _____ in?

A: _____ in aisle 3, and there _____ in the _____ section at the end of aisle 2.

B: Thank you.

A: Do you need anything else?

B: Yes, where _____ ?

A: It's at the end of aisle 1 in the _____ section. Let me show you.

| broccoli |
| low-fat milk |
| tomato soup |
| sausages |
| bread |
| oranges |
| soda |

B Present your conversation to another pair. Observe their conversation.

AT WORK ▶ Offering and asking for help

🔊 **A** Listen to different ways to ask for and offer help. Who is asking for help?
2-47 Who is offering help?

Kitchen assistant: Do you need any help?

Chef: Yes, please. Can you help me chop these vegetables?

Associate: Excuse me. I don't understand how to check out these vegetables. Could you help me?

Manager: Yes, of course. Let me show you.

B Work with a partner. Practice the conversations in A. Then take turns offering and asking for help.

C Think about it. Ask and answer the questions with a partner.

1. When do you offer help to people at work?

2. When do you ask other people to help you at work?

NEED HELP?

Could you help me, please?

Can you help me open this jar?

Can you show me how to use this machine?

▶▶TEST YOURSELF

Act out this situation with a classmate. Take turns with each role.

Salesperson: You work in a clothing store. Offer to help a customer.

Customer: You can't find the item you want. Ask for some help.

ACADEMIC

1 Build reading strategies

A Read the definitions. Complete the sentences with your own ideas.

calcium: a nutrient in food that makes bones and teeth strong

calories: the amount of energy in a food

diet: the food you eat every day

protein: a nutrient found in meat, milk, eggs, and beans

There is a lot of calcium in _____ .　　My daily diet includes a lot of _____ .

There are a lot of calories in _____ .　　There is a lot of protein in _____ .

B How many times a week do you eat these foods? Write the numbers below.

_____ fruit　　　　_____ rice　　　_____ bread

_____ chocolate　　_____ milk　　　_____ vegetables

C Preview the article. Read the title and the first two sentences. What is the purpose of this article?

D Read the article. Find the source. Where is this information from?

Good Food for Good Health

For a healthy lifestyle, it is important to eat the right foods and stay active. The USDA booklet *Dietary Guidelines for Americans* gives information and advice. A healthy eating pattern includes:

• a variety of vegetables, especially dark green, red, and orange vegetables

• fruits, especially whole fruits

• grains, especially whole grains, such as whole-wheat bread, whole-grain cereals and crackers, oatmeal, and brown rice

• fat-free or low-fat dairy products, including milk, yogurt, cheese, and soy beverages that contain a lot of calcium

• a variety of protein foods, including seafood, lean meat[1] and poultry, eggs, legumes (beans and peas), and nuts, seeds, and soy products

• oils

• very small amounts of food containing fat, sugar, or salt

Exercise is also important. For the best health benefits, adults should do one of the following:

• 150 minutes (2 hours and 30 minutes) each week of moderate physical activity (such as fast walking or tennis)

• 75 minutes (1 hour and 15 minutes) each week of vigorous[2] physical activity (such as jogging or swimming)

[1] lean meat: meat that has very little fat
[2] vigorous: energetic, high intensity
Source: *Office of Disease Prevention and Health Promotion; www.health.gov*

2-48 **E** Listen and read the article again. Which advice do you follow in your daily diet and exercise?

F Mark the sentences *T* (true) or *F* (false).

_____ 1. The dietary guidelines help people choose food for a healthy diet.

_____ 2. You should eat fruits and vegetables every day.

_____ 3. You shouldn't eat any food that has salt or sugar.

_____ 4. Adults who eat a healthy diet don't need to exercise.

G Complete the sentences. Use the words in the box.

lean	vigorous	calcium	whole-grain

1. Milk, yogurt, and cheese contain _____ .

2. You should eat more _____ bread than white bread.

3. You can eat _____ meat and fish as part of a healthy diet.

4. Running is an example of a _____ physical activity.

2 Read a nutrition label

A Read the nutrition labels. Answer the questions about each label.

Serving* Size 1 cup
Servings Per Container 2
Amount Per Serving
Calories 110
Total Fat 1.5g
Sodium 920mg
Calcium 5%

INGREDIENTS
Black beans, water, tomatoes, salt, carrots, onions, red peppers, garlic

Serving* Size 1/2 cup
Servings Per Container 3
Amount Per Serving
Calories 130
Total Fat 9g
Sodium 870mg
Calcium 0%

INGREDIENTS
Chicken broth, flour, chicken, milk, salt, oil, onions

*serving: amount of food that a person eats at one time

1. How much is one serving?

2. How many servings are in one package?

3. How many calories are in one serving?

4. Which is a better choice according to the article in 1D?

B Think about it. Talk about these questions with your classmates.

1. Why should you read nutrition labels?

2. How do the dietary guidelines in 1D help you interpret these nutrition labels?

> **READER'S NOTE**
> Apply information from your reading to real-life problems and tasks so that you will remember it and understand it better.

⏻ BRING IT TO LIFE

Look for a nutrition label on a food product at home or at the supermarket. Bring the product to class. Tell the class about the information on the label. How does it fit into the dietary guidelines for everyday foods?

A Work with a team. Look at the picture. Answer the questions.

1. How many sections are there in this store?
2. Name one kind of food in each section.
3. What food sections are missing?
4. How many customers are there? What are they doing?
5. How many workers are there? What are they doing?
6. What kinds of equipment can you see?
7. Name the types of containers that you see.

B Work with a team. Choose one person to be a supermarket assistant in your group. Take turns asking for help finding an item in the store.

A: *May I help you?*

B: *I'm looking for... Can you help me?*

A: *Yes, of course. The... are in aisle... Let me show you.*

C Role-play the supermarket workers in the picture. Ask each other for help.

D Write three true and three false sentences about the picture using *There is/There are*. Close your books. Take turns reading your sentences to the class. The other students will tell you which sentences are true and which are false.

E Interview three classmates. Write their answers in the chart.

How much/How many cups/glasses of _____ do you drink every day?
How much/How many servings of _____ do you eat every day?

Classmates' names	1.	2.	3.
Coffee or tea			
Water or juice			
Cookies or chips			
Fruit			
Rice, bread, or pasta			
Vegetables			
Dairy (milk, cheese, or yogurt)			
Meat or fish			
Beans or nuts			

F Think about the answers to the survey. Is your diet similar to your classmates' diets, or different? How can you all improve your diets?

G Write a paragraph about your diet. What do you eat every day? What's something you don't eat? How can you improve your diet? Read the example.

> I usually *eat meat every day. I like beef and chicken more than fish. I also eat a lot of dairy products and fresh fruit. I love yogurt with strawberries. I don't eat many vegetables. I should eat more carrots and beans. And I shouldn't eat so much chocolate!*

PROBLEM SOLVING AT HOME

 A Listen and read about Dee.
2-49

> I work late every day, and I don't have much time to cook. At work, I eat too many snacks and too much sugar. Chocolate and potato chips are my favorite snacks. After work, I am too tired to cook. I prepare quick foods, like a can of soup. These foods have too much salt and sugar. I know this isn't good for me, but I'm very busy.

B Work with your classmates. Answer the questions.

1. What is Dee's problem?
2. What can she do? Think of or two or three solutions to her problem.

UNIT

8 Stay Safe and Well

A LOOK AT
- Illnesses and symptoms
- Simple past with irregular verbs
- Clarifying instructions

LESSON 1 VOCABULARY

1 Learn about medications

A Show what you know. Which medications do you know?

1. antibiotic ointment
2. antacid
3. cough syrup
4. eardrops
5. antihistamine
6. pain reliever
7. recommend
8. pharmacist

I recommend these pills.

B Listen and look at the pictures. Which part of the body is each medication for?

2-50

C Listen and repeat the words from 1A.

2-51

D Write the vocabulary. Look at the pictures. Complete the sentences.

1. The _eardrops_ are for an earache.
2. The _____ is for a cough.
3. The _____ is for a headache.
4. The _____ is for a cut finger.
5. The _____ is for heartburn.
6. The _____ is for an allergy.
7. The _____ fills prescriptions.
8. The doctor _____ hot tea and rest.

E Talk to a partner. Which brands of medications you recommend?

A: *Which medication do you recommend for an earache?*
B: *I think Clear and Easy Eardrops are very good.*

2 Talk about illnesses and symptoms

A Work in a team. Match the pictures of illnesses with the symptoms below.

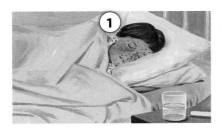
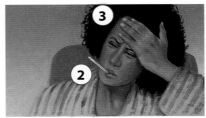

Gina has the measles.   Olivia has the flu.   Carlos is allergic to flowers.

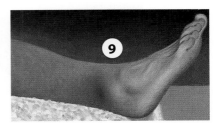

Emma has a cold.   Abdul feels sick to his stomach.   Jiang has a sprained ankle.

_____ feels dizzy   _____ has a cough   _____ has a rash

_____ feels nauseous   _____ has a fever   _____ has a runny nose

_____ is swollen   _____ has a headache   _____ is sneezing

 B Listen and check your answers.

2-52

C Complete the patient's complaint to the doctor.

Let me tell you my symptoms, Doctor. I know I have a _____ because I feel hot.
                                                        1

(Ah-choo!) I _____ and coughing all the time, plus I have a _____ nose. There's a
             2   3

red, itchy _____ on my hands and feet. In fact, my feet are so _____ I can't wear
           4   5

my shoes. And my poor stomach! I feel _____ every time I eat. Oh no! Now I feel
                                        6

_____ . I have to sit down. What's wrong with me?
   7

D Talk to a partner. Ask and answer questions. Use the pictures in 2A.

A: *What's the matter with _____ ?*   A: *What are her/his symptoms?*

B: *She/He has/feels/is _____ .*   B: *She/He has/is _____ .*

E Discuss these questions with your classmates: Which people in 2A need medical treatment? Who can get treatment at home?

▶▶ **TEST YOURSELF**

Copy the chart in your notebook. Write three illnesses. Then write two symptoms for each.

	Illness 1	Illness 2	Illness 3
Symptom 1			
Symptom 2			

1 Prepare to write

A Talk about the pictures. Which of these is a problem?
Which find problems or fix problems?

B Look at the pictures. Listen to the online review.

2-53

X-ray

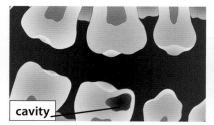

cavity

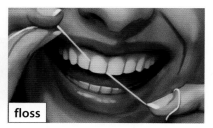

floss

braces

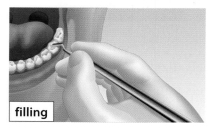

filling

C Listen again and read the review.

2-53

Greenview Dental Clinic

Review by
LINA NOVAK

★★★★★ 7/17/18

I visited this dental clinic twice last year. The first visit was for a check-up and a cleaning. First, the dental assistant took some X-rays. They showed two cavities. Then the dental hygienist cleaned my teeth. She gave me a new toothbrush and some good advice about brushing and flossing my teeth carefully. I went back again a week later and got two fillings. The dentist explained everything carefully, and the treatment didn't hurt at all. He recommended braces for my front teeth, so I scheduled a visit to an orthodontist. The staff at this dental clinic was very helpful and professional, and I didn't have to wait long. I recommend this dentist.

> **WRITER'S NOTE**
> The concluding sentences of the review summarize the writer's opinion and give reasons for the recommendation.

D Check your understanding. Mark the sentences *T* (true) or *F* (false).

_____ 1. Lina went to the dentist last year.

_____ 2. The dentist took X-rays of Lina's teeth.

_____ 3. The dental assistant filled two cavities.

_____ 4. Lina made an appointment with an orthodontist.

_____ 5. Lina had one complaint about the staff at the dental clinic.

E Listen to the voice messages and complete the appointment log.

2-54

Name of patient	Type of health care provider	Reason for visit	Medications used
	optometrist		
	chiropractor		
	dermatologist		

F Listen again and check your answers. What parts of the body do these doctors treat?

2-54

2 Plan

A Plan your ideas before you write. Copy the mind map in your notebook. Complete each section with one of the topics below.

1. Type of doctor

2. When was your visit?

3. Reasons for visit

4. Medication or treatment

5. Reasons for recommendation

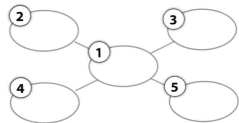

B Talk about your mind map with a partner.

3 Write about a medical visit

A Write a review of a doctor or a dentist that you visited recently.

A visit to the _____

My last appointment with a _____ was in _____ . I went to the _____ because _____ . The _____ said _____ and gave me _____ . The _____ was good because _____ . I recommend / don't recommend this _____ because _____ .

B Share your review. Read your paragraph to a partner. Compare your experiences.

▶▶ TEST YOURSELF

Complete the following sentences. Share your responses with your teacher.

1. After this writing lesson, I can…   2. I need more help with…

1 Explore the simple past of irregular verbs

🔊 2-55 **A** **Look at the pictures. Listen and read. Where are these people, and what are they talking about?**

1. **A:** What happened to Carol?

   B: She fell off her bicycle and broke her leg.

   A: That's awful! I hope she gets better soon.

2. **A:** Do you have a backache?

   B: Yes. I tried to move the sofa, and I hurt my back.

   A: That's terrible. I cut my hand with a kitchen knife. It bled a lot!

B **Analyze the simple past verbs in the conversations in 1A. Which verbs end in -ed? Which verbs don't?**

C **Study the grammar. Read the charts.**

The simple past of irregular verbs					
Affirmative statements					
I			We		
You	went	to the doctor.	You	went	to the doctor.
He/She			They		
Negative statements					
I			We		
You	didn't go	to the doctor.	You	didn't go	to the doctor.
He/She			They		

GRAMMAR NOTE

Irregular Verbs
go → went
get → got
have → had
bleed → bled
break → broke
cut → cut
fall → fell
feel → felt
hurt → hurt

D **Work with the grammar. Complete the sentences with the simple past of the words in parentheses. Which verbs are the same in the present and the past?**

1. Carol __had__ an accident. (have)

2. She _____ her leg. (break)

3. Susan _____ sick last week. (get)

4. Sam _____ his back. (hurt)

5. Amy _____ her hand. (cut)

6. Amy's hand _____ a lot. (bleed)

E Listen to the sentences about the pictures. Circle *True* or *False*.

2-56

Alan

Mariela

Tony

Jessica

| 1. True | False | 3. True | False | 5. True | False | 7. True | False |
| 2. True | False | 4. True | False | 6. True | False | 8. True | False |

F Look at the pictures in 1E. Complete the sentences with simple past verbs.

1. Alan _____ his leg. He _____ his back.

2. Mariela _____ her arm. She _____ her finger.

3. Tony _____ sick. He _____ a stomachache.

4. Jessica _____ her arm. She _____ her leg.

G Talk to a partner. Make true and false statements about the pictures in 1E. Your partner will say *true* or *false* and correct the false sentences. Then switch roles.

2 Practice: *Yes/no* questions with irregular verbs in the past

A Study the grammar. Read the chart. Listen and repeat the conversations.

2-57

Yes/no questions and answers	
A: Did you hurt your back? **B:** Yes, I did.	**A:** Did they have an accident? **B:** No, they didn't.
A: Did she cut her hand? **B:** No, she didn't.	**A:** Did he fall off his bike? **B:** Yes, he did.

B Check your understanding. Talk to a partner. Ask and answer questions about the pictures in 1E.

1. **A:** *Did Alan cut his arm?*

   B: *No, he didn't.*

2. **A:** *Did Mariela hurt her finger?*

   B: *Yes, she did.*

3 Practice: *Wh-* questions with irregular verbs in the past

🔊 **A** Study the grammar. Read the chart. Listen and repeat the conversations.
2-58

Wh- questions and answers	
A: How did you break your arm? **B:** I fell off a ladder.	**A:** How did he cut his finger? **B:** He cut himself with a kitchen knife.
A: Where did you fall? **B:** I fell in the backyard.	**A:** When did he do that? **B:** He did it last night.

B Work with the grammar. Write the questions.

1. ___How did you cut yourself___ ? I cut myself with a kitchen knife.
2. _____ ? She hurt her back lifting heavy boxes.
3. _____ ? They went to the doctor this morning.
4. _____ ? He hurt himself at the gym.
5. _____ ? She fell down the stairs and sprained her ankle.

> **GRAMMAR NOTE**
>
> We use *reflexive pronouns* when the subject and object of the action are the same.
> I cut myself.
> She hurt herself.

C Talk with a partner. Role-play a conversation with one of the people in 1E.

4 Ask questions about a workplace accident

🔊 **A** Listen to the conversation. Complete the missing information.
2-59

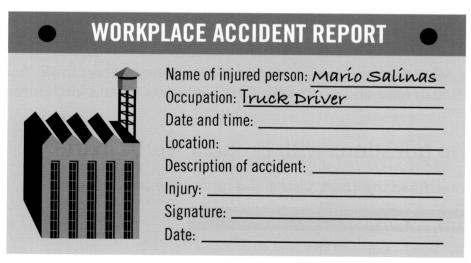

WORKPLACE ACCIDENT REPORT

Name of injured person: *Mario Salinas*
Occupation: *Truck Driver*
Date and time: _____
Location: _____
Description of accident: _____
Injury: _____
Signature: _____
Date: _____

B Talk to a partner. Ask and answer questions about the accident report in 4A.

A: *Did Mario hurt his back?*
B: *Yes, he did.*

A: *How did Mario hurt himself?*
B: *He lifted some heavy boxes.*

▶▶**TEST YOURSELF**

Imagine that your co-worker had an accident at work. Use your notebook and write five questions about the accident using the simple past.

1 Listen to learn: reading a prescription label

A Look at the prescription label with your classmates. What kind of information does the label show? Which words are new to you?

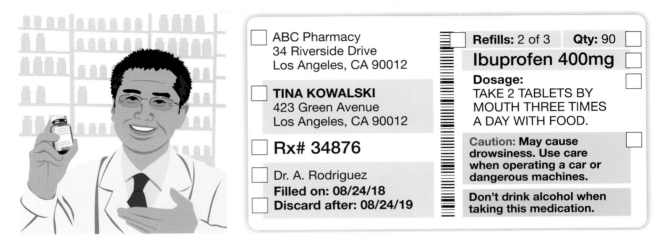

ABC Pharmacy
34 Riverside Drive
Los Angeles, CA 90012

TINA KOWALSKI
423 Green Avenue
Los Angeles, CA 90012

Rx# 34876

Dr. A. Rodriguez
Filled on: 08/24/18
Discard after: 08/24/19

Refills: 2 of 3   **Qty:** 90

Ibuprofen 400mg

Dosage:
TAKE 2 TABLETS BY
MOUTH THREE TIMES
A DAY WITH FOOD.

**Caution: May cause
drowsiness. Use care
when operating a car or
dangerous machines.**

**Don't drink alcohol when
taking this medication.**

🔊 **B** Listen. What is the pharmacist explaining?
2-60
  a. How to take this medication
  b. How to read a prescription label
  c. How to order a refill

🔊 **C** Listen again. Number the parts of the label.
2-60

D Discuss this question with your classmates:
  What parts of a prescription label are the most important?

2 Practice your pronunciation

🔊 **A** Listen to the examples. What is different in the relaxed pronunciation?
2-61

	Formal	Relaxed
have/has to	Do you *have to* take all the pills? She *has to* drink a glass of water with each pill.	How much do I *have to* pay? He *has to* go to the pharmacy after work.

B Work with a partner. Take turns reading the sentences in the box. Practice formal and relaxed pronunciation.

Do I have to take these with food?	He has to finish all the pills.
When do I have to take the medicine?	She has to stay in bed.

3 Review *have to* and *has to*

A Listen and read the conversation. Which parts of the prescription label are the questions about?

Luis: I'd like to pick up my prescription, please. My name is Luis Flores.

Pharmacist: Do you have any questions about your medication?

Luis: Yes. How many pills do I have to take a day?

Pharmacist: You have to take two pills twice a day.

Luis: Do I have to take them with food?

Pharmacist: Yes, it's very important. You **have to** take them with food.

Luis: OK. Did you say two pills once a day?

Pharmacist: No. Two pills **twice** a day.

Luis: Thank you.

B Listen and mark the answers to the questions.

1. a. Yes, he did.   b. No, he didn't.   3. a. Yes, he does.   b. No, he doesn't.

2. a. Yes, she did.   b. No, she didn't.   4. a. Yes, he does.   b. No, he doesn't.

C Think about the grammar. Look at 1A and answer these questions.

1. How do you form *wh-* questions with *have to*?

2. How do you form *yes/no* questions with *have to*?

3. How do you form third-person questions with *have to*?

D Write questions. Use *have to* or *has to*.

1. when / you / take these pills? <u>When do you have to take these pills?</u>

2. how often / he / see the doctor? _____

3. she / avoid dairy products? _____

4. he / take the pills before meals? _____

5. how long / she / take the pills? _____

6. how much / I / pay? _____

E Work in a team. Make a list of questions to ask a pharmacist about medications. Share your two best questions with the class.

F Discuss this question with your classmates:

Why is it important to ask your pharmacist questions about your medications?

4 Make conversation: clarifying prescription instructions

A Work with a partner. Make a new conversation.
Use the prescription label in 1A or your own ideas.

> **A:** I'd like to pick up my prescription, please. My name is _____ .
>
> **B:** Is your first name _____ ? What's your date of birth?
>
> **A:** Yes, that's right. And my date of birth is _____ .
>
> **B:** Your prescription is ready. You have to take _____ .
>
> **A:** Do I have to _____ ?
>
> **B:** Yes, it's very important. You have to _____ .
>
> **A:** OK. Did you say _____ ?
>
> **B:** No, you have to take _____ .
>
> **A:** OK. Thank you very much.

NEED HELP?

Frequency expressions

How often...?

once a day

twice a day

three times a day

every two hours

B Present your conversation to another pair. Observe their conversation.

AT WORK ▶ Clarifying instructions

🔊 2-64 **A** Look at the pictures and listen. Who are these people? Where are they?
What is the same about the way they clarify instructions?

> **A:** Take her temperature every three hours.
>
> **B:** Did you say I have to take her temperature every three hours?
>
> **A:** Yes, that's right.

> **A:** You have to hold your hand under cold water for four minutes, and then put a bandage on it.
>
> **B:** Do I really have to keep it in cold water for four minutes?
>
> **A:** Yes, those are the instructions.

B Work with a partner. Practice the conversations. Use your own ideas.

C Think about it. When did you need to clarify instructions at work? Tell the class.

▶▶ TEST YOURSELF

Act out this situation with a classmate. Take turns with each role.

Pharmacist: Give first-aid instructions for a burn or a cut.
Customer: Ask for clarification of the instructions.

1 Build reading strategies

A Read the definitions. Which words can you use to describe medications?

antiseptic: something that kills bacteria

first aid: basic medical treatment in an emergency

injured: hurt

supplies: things people need for their work or activities

B Look at the picture in the article in 1D. Which of these supplies is NOT in the first-aid kit?

bandages   antibiotic ointment   scissors   gloves

C Preview the article. What website is it? What page of the website is it on?

D Read the article.

prepareforemergencies.org

| HOME | DISASTERS | EMERGENCIES | FIRST AID |

Preparing a First Aid Kit

Preparing a First-Aid Kit

In an emergency, you or someone in your family might be injured. It is important to have a first-aid kit with some basic supplies. You should have one first-aid kit in your home and one in your car. Here are some things you might find in a first-aid kit.

For small cuts or burns:
- bandages of different sizes
- antibiotic ointment
- antiseptic wipes (for cleaning cuts)
- scissors (for cutting bandages)

For someone with a fever or pain:
- a thermometer (for taking a temperature)
- non-prescription medicines, such as the pain reliever acetaminophen

Where should you put your first-aid kit? It should be in a place that is easy for you to get to but where children cannot find it. It should be in a plastic box, and the box should be easy to open. Check the supplies in your first-aid kit often. Check the expiration dates of medicines.

Remember! In a serious emergency[1], you should always call emergency services. Ask them how to use first aid before the doctor or other help arrives.

[1]serious emergency: a very bad emergency
Source: *www.ready.gov*

READER'S NOTE
The navigation bar at the top of the web page includes links to different topics on the site. Text in blue links directly to another web page (often for more information or shopping).

 E Listen and read the article again.
2-65

F **Choose the correct words. Circle *a* or *b*.**

1. You can use antiseptic wipes to _____ .

   a. clean cuts   b. cut bandages

2. Acetaminophen is a _____ medicine.

   a. prescription   b. non-prescription

3. A good place for a first-aid kit is _____ .

   a. on a high shelf   b. under the bed

4. You can use first aid _____ an ambulance arrives.

   a. before   b. after

G **Complete the sentences. Use the words in the box.**

scissors	serious	thermometer	injured

1. You can take your temperature with a _____ .

2. You can use _____ for cutting bandages.

3. A first-aid kit is useful when someone is _____ .

4. In a _____ emergency, you should call 911.

2 Read a pie chart about injuries at work

A **Look at the pie chart. Answer the questions.**

1. What is the main topic of the chart?

   _____

2. What is the most common kind of injury?

   _____

3. What does the segment in light blue represent?

   _____

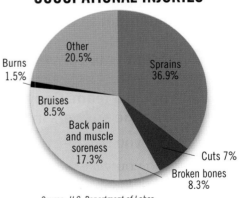

OCCUPATIONAL INJURIES

Other 20.5%
Burns 1.5%
Sprains 36.9%
Bruises 8.5%
Back pain and muscle soreness 17.3%
Cuts 7%
Broken bones 8.3%

Source: *U.S. Department of Labor*

B **Think about it. Talk about the questions with your classmates.**

1. Why do you have to report accidents at work?

2. What are some common accidents in the workplace?

3. What kinds of first-aid supplies do people use at work or school?

4. What kinds of occupations do you think have the most risk of injury?

⏻ BRING IT TO LIFE

Find information about first-aid kits on the Internet or at a pharmacy. How much do the kits cost? What's in all or most of the kits? Report the information you learned to the class.

A **Work with a team. Look at the picture. Answer the questions.**

PICK-UP

♦ **Smallgreen Pharmacy**
1818 Oak Ave
Rosemead, CA 91770
Dr. L. Luther   PHONE **555-5522**

NO **00859023–57988**   DATE **03/07/18**

Alki Elmi
345 First Street Rosemead, CA 91770

TAKE ONE TABLET BY
MOUTH 2 TIMES A DAY
AS NEEDED FOR PAIN.

NAPROXEN 500 MG

REFILLS: 2

Discard after 03/07/20

👁 May cause drowsiness.

1. Where are these people?

2. What are they doing?

3. Name three kinds of medications you might find in the pharmacy.

4. What information is on the prescription label?

B **Role-play a conversation about the prescription label in the picture. Ask and answer questions about the information. Remember to clarify instructions.**

C **Present your conversation to the other teams.**

D **Work in a team. Copy the chart below into your notebook. Interview each other. Write the answers in the chart.**

1. Do you have allergies? What are you allergic to?

2. Do you visit the doctor or dentist regularly for a check-up?

3. What over-the-counter medications do you buy regularly at the pharmacy?

	Me	Team member 2	Team member 3	Team member 4
Allergies				
Doctor/dentist check-up				
Over-the-counter				

E Write a summary and report the data to the rest of the class.

Three-quarters of our group has allergies. Everyone is allergic to different things...

F Look at the pictures. Ask and answer questions about what happened to each person and what he or she did next.

A: *What happened to this man?*
B: *He burned himself on a hot pot.*

A: *What did he do next?*
B: *He put his hand in cool water for five minutes.*

G Work with a partner. Discuss the situations. What do you have to do in each situation? Complete the chart.

	Do now	Do later
You get a small cut.		
You get a small burn.		
You feel dizzy.		
You feel nauseous.		
You sprain your ankle.		

H Compare your answers with another group. Choose the best answers.

PROBLEM SOLVING AT WORK

2-66

A Listen and read about Julio.

> Julio Gonzalez works part-time in a supermarket. He doesn't make a lot of money. Yesterday he picked up a very heavy box and hurt his shoulder. His co-worker said, "Fill out an accident report and tell the supervisor. The company has to pay when there's an accident at work." Julio didn't have time to complete an accident report because he had to pick up his kids from school. Today he's at work, but he's in terrible pain. He can't do his job. He's not sure what to do now.

B Work with your classmates. Answer the questions.

1. What is Julio's problem?
2. What can he do? Think of two or three solutions to his problem.

UNIT

9 Money Matters

A LOOK AT
- Banking and ATMs
- Purpose and reasons with *to* and *because*
- Responding to requests

LESSON 1 VOCABULARY

1 Learn about banking

A Show what you know. Circle the words you know. Which of these do you use regularly?

1. bank statement
2. checking account
3. current balance
4. personal check
5. cash
6. debit card
7. credit card bill
8. savings account

🔊 3-02 **B** Listen and look at the pictures. What is Peter doing?

🔊 3-03 **C** Listen and repeat the words from 1A.

D Write the vocabulary. Look at the pictures. Complete the sentences.

1. He has $21 in __cash__ .
2. The _____ is for $350.96.
3. There is $850 in his _____ .
4. His _____ is due by 10/19/18.
5. His credit card's _____ is $540.
6. He took out $40 with his _____ .
7. His _____ ends on 10/30/18.
8. He has $1,800 in his _____ .

E Ask and answer the questions with a partner.

1. How do you pay your bills—by check, by automatic payment, by money order, or online?
2. What's good and bad about making the minimum payment on a credit card?
3. What happens if you pay a bill late?

2 Talk about using an ATM

A Work with a partner. Match the sentences with the pictures.

 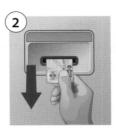 

  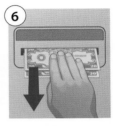

_____ Enter the amount.

_____ Enter your PIN.

_____ Insert your deposit now.

__1__ Insert your debit card for service.

_____ Remove your card.

_____ Take your cash.

B Listen and check your answers.

3-04

C Mark the sentences *T* (true) or *F* (false).

_____ 1. Peter enters his PIN first and then inserts his card.

_____ 2. Peter deposits $100 in his account.

_____ 3. Peter withdraws $60 from his checking account.

_____ 4. First, Peter takes his cash. Then he removes his card.

D Talk to a partner. Ask and answer questions about the pictures in 2A.

A: *What's Peter doing in picture #1?*

B: *He's inserting his debit card.*

E Think about it. Ask and answer the questions with your classmates.

1. Where do you usually see an ATM? Do you use an ATM? How often?

2. Which do people use most—cash, debit cards, credit cards, or personal checks?

▶▶ TEST YOURSELF

Copy the chart in your notebook. Put words from the lesson in the chart.

Ways to spend money	Ways to check your money	Verbs for using an ATM

1 Prepare to write

A Jian wants to buy a new computer. What do you think is the best order to do these things? Number the items.

_____ go to a store   _____ decide on a budget

_____ make a list of features   _____ check prices

🔊 3-05 **B** Look at the pictures. Listen to the paragraph.

🔊 3-05 **C** Listen again and read the paragraph.

> **Buying a computer**
>
> Last week, I decided to buy a new computer. First I looked at flyers from different stores and decided how much to spend. Next I made a list of all the features that I wanted, such as a good graphics card and plenty of memory. Then I went to a large electronics store to try out some of the computers. I asked the assistant for some advice too. After that, I went online to check prices on a comparison website. The website shows you the best deals. Finally I bought the computer online. I was happy because I got a real bargain!

WRITER'S NOTE
Use sequence words to show the different steps in a series of actions: _First, Next, Then, After that, Finally._

D Check your understanding. Mark the sentences _T_ (true) or _F_ (false).

_____ 1. Jian wants to buy a new computer.

_____ 2. He goes to a computer store first.

_____ 3. He talks with the store assistant about computers.

_____ 4. He saved money by shopping online.

3-06
E Listen and complete the budget. Nina bought some equipment for her home office. How much money did she spend on each item?

F Work with a partner. Ask and answer questions about Nina's budget.

A: How much did she spend on a desk?

B: She spent $200 on a desk.

Home office equipment budget

desk _____

chair _____

computer _____

printer _____

lamp _____

2 Plan

A Copy the chart into your notebook. Answer the questions.

1. When did you last purchase a large item such as a computer or furniture? What did you buy?

2. What steps did you take before buying it? Did you look online or in a catalog? Did you compare prices?

3. How did you decide what to buy? Where did you buy it?

4. How much did you spend? Did you stay within your budget? Were you happy with your purchase?

1		
2 Step 1	Step 2	Step 3
3	4	

B Talk to your partner about your purchase. Ask questions to help your partner add more details to his or her chart.

3 Write

A Write a paragraph about your shopping experience. Use the answers to your questions in 2A.

Buying a _____

Last _____ , I decided to buy a _____ .

First I _____ because I wanted to _____ .

Then I _____ . After that, I _____ . Finally I

_____ . I spent _____ and I am happy because

_____ .

B Share your writing. Read your paragraph to a partner.

▶▶ TEST YOURSELF

Complete the following sentences. Share your responses with your teacher.

1. After this writing lesson, I can…   2. I need more help with…

1 Explore purpose and reasons with *to* and *because*

🔊 **A** **Look at the picture. Listen and read.**
3-07 **Why is Nina upset?**

Karen: What are you doing?

Nina: I'm calling customer service.

Karen: Why are you calling?

Nina: To complain about this delivery.

Karen: Why are you complaining?

Nina: Because this is the wrong chair. It's too small.

B **Analyze the conversation in 1A. Underline two ways to answer the question *Why?***

C **Study the grammar. Read the charts.**

To + verb and *because*		
Purpose with *to* + verb		
She went to the store	to buy	a computer.
		some office chairs.

Reasons with *because*			
She returned	the computer	because	it was the wrong one.
	the office chairs		they were too small.

D **Work with the grammar. Complete the sentences. Use *to* or *because*.**

1. Nina called customer service __*to*__ complain about the delivery.

2. She was upset _____ they delivered the wrong chair.

3. She bought the chair online _____ it was cheaper.

4. She went online _____ compare prices.

5. She sent the chair back _____ it was too small.

E **Complete the sentences. Use *it* or *they*.**

1. I want to return these bookcases because _____ are too small.

2. She didn't like the desk because _____ was too high.

3. He bought a new camera because _____ was on sale.

4. The employees didn't like the new offices because _____ were too dark.

2 Practice: purpose and reasons with *to* and *because*

A Listen to the statements about the pictures. Circle *True* or *False*.
3-08

Bianca

1. True   False
2. True   False

Amir

3. True   False
4. True   False

Lily

5. True   False
6. True   False

B Complete the sentences about the pictures. Use the words in the box.

wants to buy a computer	is going to a job interview	buy a suit
make a deposit	got a paycheck	compare prices

1. Bianca went to the ATM to _____ because she _____ .
2. Amir went to the store to _____ because he _____ .
3. Lily went online to _____ because she _____ .

C Work with a partner. Ask and answer questions using the information in A and B. Follow the example.

A: *Why did Bianca go to the ATM?*

B: *To make a deposit.*

A: *Why did she make a deposit?*

B: *Because she got a paycheck.*

3 Practice using adjectives with *too* and *not...enough*

A Study the grammar. Listen and repeat.
3-09

too + adjective	*not* + adjective + *enough*
This coat is too small.	It's not big enough.
These chairs are too expensive.	They're not cheap enough.

GRAMMAR NOTE

It's *very* expensive. =
It costs a lot of money.
It's *too* expensive. =
I can't afford it.

B Check your understanding. Write sentences with the same meaning.
Use *too* or *enough*.

1. The phone is too big. (small) __It's not small enough.__

2. The chairs are too tall. (low) _____

3. The desk is too low. (high) _____

4. The shelves are not long enough. (short) _____

5. The rooms are not sunny enough. (dark) _____

C Work with a partner. Look at the flyer. Talk about the items.
Say why you want or don't want to buy them.

A: *Do you want to buy the cell phone?*

B: *No, I don't. This one is too expensive, and the screen isn't big enough.*

D Talk with a partner. Talk about a time you bought something and returned it.
Explain why.

4 Practice talking about reasons

A List three items that you want to buy. Next to each item, write a reason
why you want to buy it.

Item 1 _____   reason _____

Item 2 _____   reason _____

Item 3 _____   reason _____

B Work with your classmates. Try to find someone who wants to buy the same thing.
Are their reasons similar to yours or different?

▶▶ TEST YOURSELF

Close your book. Write three sentences about purchases you made. What did you buy and why?
State your purpose with *to* + verb and reasons with *because*.

1 Listen to learn: returning items to a store

A **Look at the pictures. Read the sales receipt. Then circle *a* or *b*.**

1. *Get a refund* means _____ .
   a. get your money back
   b. choose another item

2. *Exchange* means _____ .
   a. get your money back
   b. choose another item

3. The customer can get a refund _____ .
   a. on 1/20/18
   b. on 11/20/18

refund

exchange

```
CLOTHING SUPERSTORE
Date 1/15/18
Coat      $124.99
Tax       $8.74
Total     $133.73

Credit card no.
XXXXXXXXXXXX0217
Signature: Lisa Carter

Remember! Keep your
receipt. You can get
a refund or exchange
any purchase within
14 days from the
original date of
purchase.
```

B 🔊 3-10 **Listen to the three conversations. Complete the return forms.**

①

Clothing Superstore
☐ Refund
☐ Exchange
Reason for return:
_____
_____
_____

②

Clothing Superstore
☐ Refund
☐ Exchange
Reason for return:
_____
_____
_____

③

Clothing Superstore
☐ Refund
☐ Exchange
Reason for return:
_____
_____
_____

C **Discuss this question with your classmates:**

What are some situations when you cannot get a refund?

2 Practice your pronunciation

A 🔊 3-11 **Listen to the pronunciation of *I like* and *I'd like*. Then repeat the sentences.**

1. a. I like the blue socks.
   b. I'd like the blue socks.

2. a. I like new books.
   b. I'd like new books.

B 🔊 3-12 **Listen. Do you hear *I like* or *I'd like*? Circle *a* or *b*.**

1. a. I like   b. I'd like
2. a. I like   b. I'd like
3. a. I like   b. I'd like
4. a. I like   b. I'd like
5. a. I like   b. I'd like
6. a. I like   b. I'd like

C **Write four sentences with *I like* or *I'd like*. Read your sentences to a partner. Your partner will say *a* or *b*. Then change roles.**

A: *I'd like a sandwich.*

B: *It was "b."*

3 Practice polite requests and questions with *would like*

3-13

A Listen and read the conversation. Which phrase means the same as *I want*?

Clerk:	How can I help you?
Customer:	Hello. I'd like to return these bowls, please.
Clerk:	Certainly. Why are you returning them?
Customer:	Because they're the wrong size.
Clerk:	Would you like a refund or an exchange?
Customer:	I'd like to exchange them for smaller ones.
Clerk:	Do you have your sales receipt?
Customer:	Yes, here it is.

3-14

B Listen to the statements. Circle *True* or *False*.

1. True   False
2. True   False
3. True   False
4. True   False
5. True   False
6. True   False

C Think about the grammar. Look at the conversation and circle the answers.

1. We use (*Would you like* / *I'd like*) to make a polite request.
2. We use (*Would you like* / *I'd like*) to ask a polite question.

3-15

D Study the grammar. Listen and repeat the sentences.

Would like (+noun)	*Would like* (+verb)
I'd like a refund, please.	I'd like to exchange them, please.
Would you like a refund?	Would you like to exchange them for something else?
Would like = want	
Would like is more polite than *want*.	

E Talk to a partner. Make conversations for each situation.

1. The coat is too big.
2. The pants are too short.
3. The sweater is too long.

A: *I'd like to return this coat. It's too big.*

B: *Would you like a refund or an exchange?*

A: *I'd like to exchange it for a smaller one, please.*

4 Make conversation: returning and exchanging items

A Work with a partner. Make a new conversation.

A: How can I help you?

B: Hello. I'd like _____ , please.

A: Certainly. Why _____ ?

B: Because _____ .

B: Would you like _____ or _____ ?

A: I'd like _____ , please.

B: Do you have your _____ ?

A: Yes, I do. Here it is.

B Present your conversation to another pair. Observe their conversation. Do they sound polite?

AT WORK Responding to customer requests

3-16

A Listen to the conversations. What kind of request does each person make? How does the worker respond?

A: I'd like to change my appointment, please.

B: That's no problem. _____

A: I'd like to cancel my reservation, please.

B: Yes, of course. _____

B Work with a partner. Practice the conversations in A. Continue the conversations using your own ideas.

▶▶ TEST YOURSELF

Act out these situations with a classmate. Take turns with each situation: in a restaurant; in a computer store; in a furniture store.

Customer: Make a polite request.
Clerk: Respond with a polite question.

1 Build reading strategies

A Read the sentences. Match the words in bold with the definitions.

1. It's convenient to use a credit card for major **purchases**.
2. It's important to **keep** your credit card **safe**.
3. Could you **give** me some money? I'll **return** it tomorrow.
4. Stealing someone's credit card is **a type of illegal activity**.

____ fraud

____ lend

____ protect

____ transactions

B Preview the web page. Locate the bullet points. What is their purpose?

C Read the web page. Who is the information for?

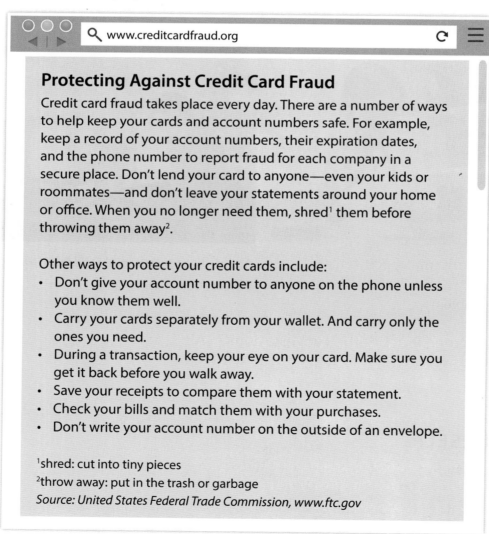

Protecting Against Credit Card Fraud

Credit card fraud takes place every day. There are a number of ways to help keep your cards and account numbers safe. For example, keep a record of your account numbers, their expiration dates, and the phone number to report fraud for each company in a secure place. Don't lend your card to anyone—even your kids or roommates—and don't leave your statements around your home or office. When you no longer need them, shred[1] them before throwing them away[2].

Other ways to protect your credit cards include:
- Don't give your account number to anyone on the phone unless you know them well.
- Carry your cards separately from your wallet. And carry only the ones you need.
- During a transaction, keep your eye on your card. Make sure you get it back before you walk away.
- Save your receipts to compare them with your statement.
- Check your bills and match them with your purchases.
- Don't write your account number on the outside of an envelope.

[1]shred: cut into tiny pieces
[2]throw away: put in the trash or garbage
Source: United States Federal Trade Commission, www.ftc.gov

READER'S NOTE
A bulleted list helps the reader to identify separate points more easily. But don't forget that the introductory paragraph contains information to help you understand the context.

D Listen and read the article again. Do you do any of these things?

E Find these sentences in the article. What do the underlined words refer to? Circle *a* or *b*.

1. When you no longer need <u>them</u>, shred them.

   a. credit cards   b. statements

2. Make sure you get <u>it</u> back before you walk away.

   a. your card   b. your transaction

3. And carry only <u>the ones</u> you need.

   a. the numbers   b. the cards

4. Check your bills and match <u>them</u> with your purchases.

   a. the receipts   b. your cards

F According to the article, are these good ideas or bad ideas? Check (✓) the correct boxes.

	Good idea	Bad idea
1. Peter keeps his credit cards in his wallet.		
2. Mary never carries more than one card. She leaves the others at home in a safe place.		
3. Julio uses a credit card, but he never keeps his receipts.		
4. Fatima cuts up her old credit card statements into very small pieces.		

2 Read a pie chart

A Read the pie chart. Answer the questions.

1. What is the main idea of the pie chart?
2. What does 37% describe?
3. Which kind of fraud happens more often: using stolen cards or using stolen information?

B Think about it. Talk about these questions with your classmates.

1. How do you think people steal credit card information?
2. Why do you think online credit card fraud is so common?
3. What can you do to protect your credit card from online fraud?

U.S. CREDIT CARD FRAUD BY TYPE, 2014

lost or stolen [2] 14% — other 4% — online (stolen card information) 45% — counterfeit [1] 37%

1. counterfeit: a copy, not real   2. stolen: taken from you illegally

Source: *www.creditcards.com*

 BRING IT TO LIFE

Find an application for a credit card or a bank account, and bring it to class. Talk about it with your classmates. What information do you need to complete the application?

TEAMWORK & LANGUAGE REVIEW

A Work with a team. Look at the picture. Answer the questions.

1. Where are these people?

2. What are they doing? Why are they here?

3. What different kinds of stores are here?

4. What products or services can you buy in each store?

B Write a conversation of 6–8 lines between a customer and an assistant in one of the stores in the picture.

C Share your conversation with another team.

D Interview the people on your team. Ask questions about a time when they returned something to a store. Complete the chart with their answers.

	Name	Name	Name
What type of store was it?			
What item did you return?			
What was wrong with the item?			
Did you get a refund or an exchange?			

E Work with your team. Role-play one of the situations you described in D. Present your role-play to the class.

F **Work in a team. You are planning a class party. You have a budget of $150.**

1. Complete the chart by choosing items from the box.

2. Decide how much or how many of each item you will need.

3. Estimate how much you will spend on each item.

4. Decide where you will purchase the items.

5. Choose who is responsible for purchasing each category of item.

balloons	cake	CD player	CDs	plastic forks
flowers	ice cream	peanuts	pizza	streamers
napkins	paper plates	soda	tablecloths	chips

Party budget planner

	Item	Quantity	Estimated cost	Place to purchase	Person responsible
Food					
Drinks					
Paper goods					
Decorations					
Entertainment					

G **Work together to write a report to summarize your plan.**

> We're planning a class party. We have a budget of $150. We'll spend $75 on pizza and ice cream. Miranda will go to the supermarket to buy the food. We'll also buy…

H **Read your report to the class. Listen carefully for differences between your plans. Which team has the best plan?**

PROBLEM SOLVING

3-18

A **Listen and read about Pavel.**

> Pavel has five credit cards. He uses his credit cards because he doesn't like to carry cash. But he doesn't keep his receipts, and sometimes he spends too much. Then he gets a big credit card bill at the end of the month.

B **Talk to your classmates. Answer the questions.**

1. What is Pavel's problem?

2. What should he do? Think of two or three solutions to his problem.

UNIT

10 Steps to Citizenship

A LOOK AT
- Citizenship and government
- *Must* and adverbs of frequency
- Making polite commands

LESSON 1 VOCABULARY

1 Learn about citizenship

A Show what you know. What kind of information is in these documents?

1. citizenship requirements
2. green card
3. application for naturalization
4. citizenship test
5. oath of allegiance
6. passport

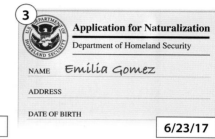

B Listen and look at the pictures. How long did it take for Emilia to become a U.S. citizen?

3-19

C Listen and repeat the words from 1A.

3-20

D Write the vocabulary. Complete the sentences.

1. Emilia met all the <u>citizenship requirements</u>.
2. Emilia got her _____ in May 2012.
3. She filled out the _____ in June 2017.
4. She took the _____ on May 7, 2018.
5. She took the _____ on July 18, 2018.
6. She got her U.S. _____ in October 2018.

E Work with a partner. Ask and answer the questions.

1. What are the steps to getting U.S. citizenship?
2. What is the most difficult part of the application process?
3. What are the benefits of U.S. citizenship?

2 Talk about government officials

A Work in a group. Match the words with the pictures.

Federal government

State government

Local government

_____ city council	_____ mayor	_____ vice president
_____ Congress	<u>1</u> president	_____ City Hall
_____ governor	_____ U.S. representative	_____ State House
_____ lieutenant governor	_____ U.S. senator	_____ White House

B Listen and check your answers.
3-21

C Talk to a partner about the pictures in 2A. Ask where each person works.

A: *Where does the U.S. senator work?*

B: *He works in Congress.*

D Talk to a partner. Ask and answer questions about your government officials.

1. Who is the _____ of the United States?
2. Who are the _____ for your state?
3. Who is the _____ of your state?
4. Who is the _____ of your city?

E Think about it. Ask and answer the questions with your classmates.

1. How can you contact your state government officials?
2. What are their roles and responsibilities?

▶▶TEST YOURSELF

Copy the chart in your notebook.
Put words from the lesson in the chart.

Federal government officials	State government officials

1 Prepare to write

A Look at the pictures. Who are the people in each picture? What are they doing?

🔊 3-22 **B** Look at the pictures. Listen to the story.

🔊 3-22 **C** Listen again and read the story.

Helping in my Community
by Sharma Robinson

My children go to Riverdale High School. The school doesn't have enough money for new science equipment. I went to a meeting of the Parent-Teacher Association (PTA). We needed to raise a lot of money.

We decided to have a bake sale to raise money. I organized the volunteers. We made cookies and cakes. Local supermarkets donated cupcakes and donuts too.

In the end, we raised over $500! At the next PTA meeting, the committee members voted for me to be the new treasurer. I am so excited to help our school and our community.

> **WRITER'S NOTE**
> Each paragraph in the story is about a new idea.
> Paragraph 1:
> What was the problem?
> Paragraph 2:
> What did they do?
> Paragraph 3:
> What was the result?

D Check your understanding. Mark the sentences *T* (true) or *F* (false).

_____ 1. Sharma is a parent.

_____ 2. Businesses donated money.

_____ 3. They sold cookies at the PTA meeting.

_____ 4. Sharma will be the next PTA president.

🔊 3-23 **E** Listen and complete the sentences in the chart.

What was the problem?	What did they do?	What was the result?
The school _____ money for new equipment.	The PTA _____ a bake sale. Sharma _____ .	They _____ for the school. The PTA _____ for Sharma to be the treasurer.

F Compare sentences with your partner. Listen again and check your work.

2 Plan

A Check (✓) the activities you have tried. Write an X for the ones you want to try. Add one idea.

- ☐ Clean up trash in your neighborhood
- ☐ Donate clothes and food to a charity
- ☐ Paint or repair a community building
- ☐ Collect money for homeless people
- ☐ Help an older person or neighbor
- ☐ _____

B Think about a time when you helped someone in your community. Ask and answer the questions with a partner.

1. What was the problem?
2. How did you help? What did you do?
3. What were the benefits for your community and for you?

C Draw the chart from 1E in your notebook. Complete it with information from the questions in 2B.

3 Write

A Write a story about a time when you or a friend helped someone in your community.

> Helping in my Community
>
> There was a problem in my community because _____ . Our neighborhood needed _____ and _____ .
>
> I decided to _____ . First, I _____ and _____ . After that, _____ .
>
> In the end, _____ . The _____ was a big success, and we were _____ . Afterwards, _____ said "_____ ." I felt _____ . I like to help in the community because _____ .

B Share your writing. Read your story to a partner. Ask for some suggestions or advice.

▶▶ TEST YOURSELF

Complete the following sentences. Share your responses with your teacher.

1. After this writing lesson, I can…
2. I need more help with…

1 Explore using *must* and *must not*

A Look at the pictures. Read the rules. Which rules are for pedestrians? Which are for drivers?

You must stop at a red light.

You must not go over the speed limit.

You must not cross the street in the middle of the block.

You must wait for the walk signal.

B Analyze the sentences in 1A. What word means the same as *have to*?

C Study the grammar. Read the charts. How is the negative of *must* different from other verbs?

Must and *must not*					
Affirmative statements					
I You He She	must	stop.	We You They	must	stop.

Negative statements					
I You He She	must not	cross here.	We You They	must not	cross here.

D Work with the grammar. Complete the sentences. Use *must (not)* and the verbs in parentheses.

1. Drivers __must stop__ at a red light. (stop)

2. Drivers _____ on the sidewalk. (drive)

3. Car passengers _____ a seat belt. (wear)

4. Pedestrians _____ in the street. (walk)

E Work with a partner. Write four more rules for drivers and pedestrians. Use *must* or *must not*.

2 Practice statements with *must* and *must not*

A Read the rules. Mark the sentences *T* (true) or *F* (false). Change the false sentences. Make them true.

> **Rules on the bus:**
>
> Don't talk to the bus driver.
> Stand behind the yellow line.
> No food or drink.
> No radios.
> Exact change only.

    _F_ 1. Passengers must ^{not} talk to the driver.

    _____ 2. Passengers must stand behind the yellow line.

    _____ 3. Passengers must eat and drink on the bus.

    _____ 4. Passengers must listen to radios.

    _____ 5. Passengers must give the driver exact change.

B Look at the signs. Write sentences with *must* or *must not*.

1.   You must not park here.

2. _____

3. _____

4. _____

3 Practice using *must* with adverbs of frequency

🔊
3-24

A Study the grammar. Listen and repeat.

Must + adverb
You must always stop at a stop sign.
You must usually pay a fine for speeding.
You must never drive through a red light.

0% never   usually   100% always

B Check your understanding. Add *must* and *always*, *usually*, or *never* to each sentence. What are the rules in your state?

1. Drivers _____ stop when they see an ambulance.

2. Cyclists _____ stay in the bicycle lane.

3. Drivers _____ have a driver's license in their car.

4. Young children _____ sit in a safety seat in a car.

5. Drivers _____ have car insurance.

6. Cyclists _____ ride a bicycle without a helmet.

7. Drivers _____ pay to park in the city center.

8. Cyclists _____ cycle on a highway.

C Talk to a partner. Discuss your answers to 1B. Do you always follow these rules?

🔊 **D** Listen to a manager explaining the office regulations to a new employee.
3-25   Complete the poster with the rules.

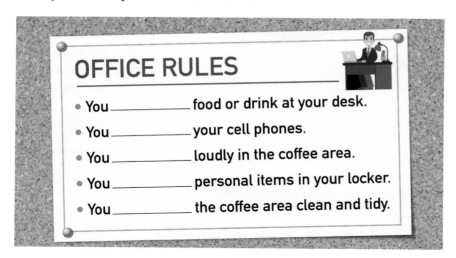

OFFICE RULES

• You _____ food or drink at your desk.

• You _____ your cell phones.

• You _____ loudly in the coffee area.

• You _____ personal items in your locker.

• You _____ the coffee area clean and tidy.

E Look at the poster. Talk with a partner. Do you think these rules are good or bad?
Do you always, usually, or never follow these rules in your workplace or at school?

4 Practice talking about rules in your community

A Work in pairs. Write five new rules for your community.

New rules for our community	Why these rules are good
1. You must not drop litter in the street.	The streets will be cleaner.
2.	
3.	
4.	
5.	

B Join with another pair. Explain why your rules are a good idea.

A: *What is your new rule for our community?*

B: *Our new rule is: You must not drop litter in the street.*

A: *Why is that a good rule?*

B: *Because the streets will be cleaner.*

▶▶ **TEST YOURSELF**

Close your book. Use your notebook. Write three new rules for your classroom. Read your rules
to a partner.

You must never be late for class.

1 Listen to learn: forms of ID

A **Look at the pictures. When do you need these forms of identification?**

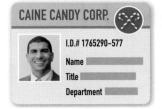

driver's license and registration

work ID card

college ID

transit pass

B **Listen to four conversations. Who is asking for the ID in each conversation? Write the correct number.**

3-26

_____ police officer   _____ security guard

_____ administrative assistant   _____ train conductor

C **Listen again. Circle the problem in each conversation.**

3-26

1. expired	no photo	no ID
2. speeding	parking	broken taillight
3. no signature	expired	wrong card
4. no ID	wrong card	expired

D **Discuss this question with a partner:**

In what kinds of jobs do you need to ask for someone's ID?

2 Practice your pronunciation

A **Listen to the intonation of these responses. What differences do you notice?**

3-27

A: Could I see your driver's license, please?   **B:** Yes, of course. (He sounds polite)

                                                         B: Yes, of course. (He sounds upset.)

B **Listen to the intonation. Do they sound polite or upset? Circle the answers.**

3-28

1. Do you need to see my driver's license?   polite   upset
2. Is there a problem with my car registration? polite   upset
3. Yes, certainly.   polite   upset
4. OK. Here they are.   polite   upset

C **Work with a partner. Read the sentences in 2B. Your partner will decide if you are polite or upset.**

3 Practice using *must* and *should*

 A Listen and read the conversation. Identify one rule and one piece of advice.

3-29

Officer: May I see your license and registration, sir?
Driver: Of course, Officer. Here they are. What's the problem?

Officer: Did you know that your left taillight is broken?
Driver: No, I didn't.
Officer: You must not drive with a broken taillight.

Officer: You should check your tires too. This one looks flat.
Driver: Yes. I'll take care of it right away.
Officer: Thank you, sir. Have a good day.

B Listen and mark the answers to the questions.

3-30

1. a. Yes, she did. b. No, she didn't.   3. a. Yes, she did. b. No, she didn't.
2. a. Yes, he did.   b. No, he didn't.   4. a. Yes, he did.   b. No, he didn't.

C Think about the grammar. Read the rules and advice in the chart. Do you use *should* for rules or for advice?

Rules (It's the law!)	Advice (It's a good idea.)
You must wear a seat belt.	You should check your car engine regularly.
You must not drink alcohol and drive.	You should not play loud music in your car.

D Work with a partner. Is it the law? Complete the sentences. Use *must (not)* or *should (not)*.

1. You _____ check your tires every month.
2. You _____ have your registration in your car.
3. You _____ drive and text at the same time.
4. You _____ eat and drive at the same time.
5. You _____ drive a car without insurance.
6. You _____ have a GPS in your car.

4 Make conversation: responding politely to a police officer

A **Work with a partner. Make new conversations. Choose from the situations in the box.**

A: Good afternoon. May I see your _____ ?

B: Of course, Officer. Here it is.

A: Did you know that _____ ?

B: No, I didn't.

A: You _____ .

B: Thank you. I'll _____ right away.

A: Thank you. Have a good day.

NEED HELP?

I'll check the _____ carefully next time.
I'll be more careful next time.
I won't do that again.

front tire is flat	brake lights aren't working
turned right at a "no right turn" sign	didn't stop at a crosswalk
parked in the wrong place	inspection sticker is expired
driving 30mph in a 20mph zone	didn't stop at a stop sign

B **Present your conversation to another pair. Observe their conversation.**

AT WORK ▶ Making polite commands

🔊 **A** **Look at the pictures. Listen to the conversations. What is the problem in each situation?**
3-31

May I see your ID, please?

May I see your driver's license, please?

Could I see your bag, please?

B **Work with a partner. Look at the pictures again. Role-play the two people in each picture. Solve the problems politely. Then present the role-play to your class.**

A: *Good afternoon. May I see your ID, please?*

B: *Of course...*

▶▶ TEST YOURSELF

Act out this situation with a classmate. Take turns with each role.

Visitor: You are entering a government building.
Security guard: You need to check the visitor's identification.

ACADEMIC

1 Build reading strategies

A Read the sentences and look at the words in bold. Which of these words describes a section of an organization? A person? A place?

A **judge** makes decisions about the law.

A judge works in a **court**.

The Supreme Court is the judicial **branch** of government.

Justice Sonia Sotomayor, a judge on the Supreme Court

B Preview the article. Look carefully at the pictures and the headings. What kind of information do they give?

C Read the article. How many types of public officials are named?

The Three Branches of Government

There are three branches of the U.S. government: the Executive Branch, the Legislative Branch, and the Judicial Branch.

The Executive Branch is composed of [1] the president, vice president, and Cabinet members. The president is the leader of the government and the military. He signs new laws for the whole country. The vice president is in second place after the president. The president chooses Cabinet members to be in charge of [2] various departments such as health or education.

The Legislative Branch, or Congress, is composed of two parts: the Senate and the House of Representatives. There are 100 senators in the Senate and 435 representatives in the House of Representatives. Congress makes new laws for the country and decides the budget.

The Judicial Branch is composed of the Supreme Court and the federal courts. They explain the laws. There are nine judges on the Supreme Court. The president chooses them, and they are approved by the Senate. The Supreme Court is the highest court in the United States.

[1] composed of: made up of
[2] in charge of: responsible for

3-32 **D** Listen and read the article again. What role does each branch of the U.S. government have in making new laws?

E These sentences are false. Make them true.

1. The ~~vice~~ president is the leader of the country.

2. The president makes new laws for the country.

3. The Cabinet is part of the judicial branch.

4. There are 100 representatives in the House of Representatives.

5. There are six judges on the Supreme Court.

F Complete the sentences. Use the words in the box.

branches	composed	laws	leader	judges

1. The president is the _____ of the country.

2. The president signs new _____ .

3. The Supreme Court has nine _____ .

4. Congress is _____ of two parts.

5. The U.S. government has three _____ .

2 Read about government officials

A Read the chart. Circle the correct years in the sentences below.

	President	U.S Senator	U.S. Representative	Supreme Court Judge
How long is a term?	4 years	6 years	2 years	For life*
How many terms can he or she serve?	2 terms	No limit	No limit	

* The judges are on the Supreme Court until they die or decide to retire.

1. Senator Jones was elected in 2010. His term ended in (2014 / 2016).

2. Representative Smith was elected in 2016. Her term ended in (2017 / 2018).

3. The president was elected in 2012. His term ended in (2016 / 2020).

READER'S NOTE

Use the information in the chart to help you understand the article in 1C. Combining information from different sources can help you understand it better.

B Think about it. Talk about these questions with your classmates.

1. Would you like to be a government official? Why or why not?

2. What are three questions you would like to ask the president?

3. Based on the information in the article and the chart, what branch of government would you like to serve in and for how long?

⏻ BRING IT TO LIFE

Brainstorm a list of questions about the U.S. government with your classmates. Find the answer to one question on the Internet or in the library. Talk about the answers with your class.

TEAMWORK & LANGUAGE REVIEW

A Work with a team. Look at the pictures. Ask and answer the questions.

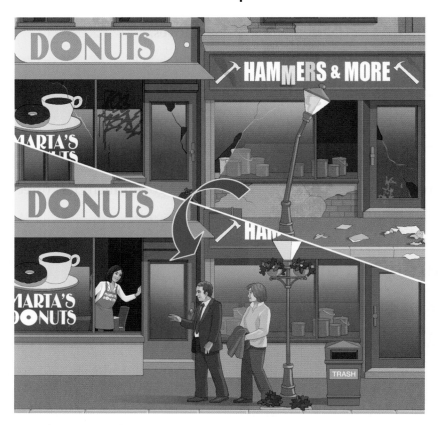

1. What kind of businesses are in the picture?

2. What problems can you see in the first picture?

3. How do you think the store owners feel about these problems?

4. What are the differences in the second picture?

5. How do you think these store owners solved their problems?

6. How can neighbors work together to solve problems in the community?

7. Which government officials could you contact to help solve community problems?

B Write a conversation of 6–8 lines between the people in the picture. Share your conversations with your classmates.

A: Hi Marta, how's business?

B: We're doing well, thank you! What do you think of our street?

C Work with your team. Make a list of five rules to help keep your neighborhood safe and clean. Then present your list to the class.

You must not drop trash in the street.

D Work with your class. Decide which rules are the best for your neighborhood. Work together to make a poster with the ten best rules. Add illustrations or diagrams for some of the rules.

E Interview three classmates about their participation in the community. Write their answers in the chart. Why did they choose each activity? What are its benefits for the community?

A: *How do you participate in the community?*

B: *Well, I volunteer at...*

	Classmate 1	Classmate 2	Classmate 3
Volunteer			
Go to city council meetings			
Go to PTA meetings			
Read a local newspaper			
Other: _____			

F Report the answers to your class. Discuss the benefits of participating in the community.

Tam often goes to city council meetings. He thinks it's good because...

G Choose two issues that are important in your community right now. Complete the sentences. Remember to give a reason for your opinion.

I think that we should...

In my opinion, the city should...

PROBLEM SOLVING

3-33

A Listen and read about Kemal.

> Kemal drove past a school last week at 45 miles per hour. The speed limit there is 20 miles per hour. A police officer stopped him and gave him a ticket for speeding. He has to pay $150 for the ticket, but he doesn't have the money right now. What will he say to the judge when he goes to court?

B Work with your classmates. Answer the questions.

1. What is Kemal's problem?

2. What can he do? Think of three solutions to his problem.

C Role-play the conversation between Kemal and the judge. Remember to use polite intonation.

11 Deal with Difficulties

A LOOK AT
- Emergencies and disasters
- Past continuous
- Making an emergency call

LESSON 1 VOCABULARY

1 Learn about crimes and emergencies

A Show what you know. Which words do you know? Which of these situations are crimes and which are emergencies?

1. robbery
3. vandalism
5. accident
2. mugging
4. power outage
6. explosion

B Listen and look at the pictures. Identify the location of each situation.
3-34

C Listen and repeat the words from 1A.
3-35

D Write the vocabulary. Complete the sentences.

1. There was an _accident_ on the highway.
2. There was a _____ in the store.
3. There was _____ on the corner of Park Street and 3rd Avenue.
4. There was an _____ in the factory.
5. There was a _____ in front of the bank.
6. There was a _____ in the subway.

E Talk with a partner. Ask and answer questions about the pictures in 1A.

A: *What's happening in picture 1?*
B: *There's a robbery. Someone is stealing money from the cash register.*

2 Talk about natural disasters

A Work in a team. Match the words with the pictures.

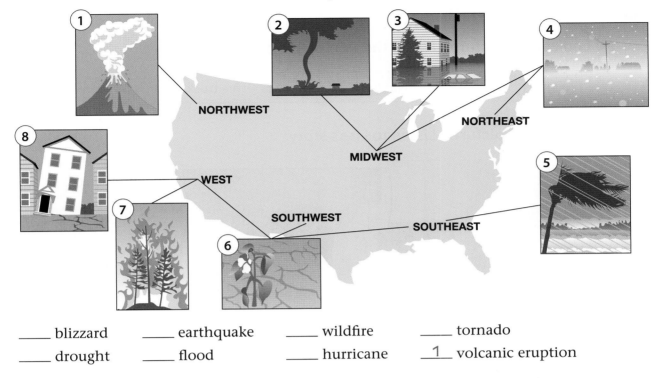

_____ blizzard	_____ earthquake	_____ wildfire	_____ tornado
_____ drought	_____ flood	_____ hurricane	_1_ volcanic eruption

B Listen and check your answers.

3-36

C Complete the sentences. Use words from 2A.

1. 1906: Many buildings fell during an __earthquake__ in San Francisco.

2. 1930s: The Midwest had a 10-year _____ . There was very little rain.

3. 1980: Fire and smoke came from a _____ at Mount St. Helens.

4. 1992: A _____ in Florida had winds of 145 miles per hour.

5. 1993: Over forty inches of snow fell during a _____ in the Northeast.

6. 2005: Water from a _____ covered roads and bridges in New Jersey.

7. 2007: In California, _____ burned over 1,000,000 acres of land.

8. 2011: On April 25–28th, there were 362 _____ in the Midwest.

D Think about it. Ask and answer the questions with your classmates.

1. What emergencies or natural disasters occur in your city or state?

2. Do the emergencies and natural disasters occur at a certain time of year?

3. Can you think of any recent natural disasters or emergencies in the U.S.?

▶▶ **TEST YOURSELF**

Use your notebook. Copy this chart. Put the words from this lesson in the chart.

Crimes	Emergencies	Natural disasters

1 Prepare to write

A Look at the pictures. Name the things and people you see.

| firefighter | smoke | neighbor | window | fire truck |

3-37
B Look at the pictures. Listen to Lisa's story.

3-37
C Listen again and read Lisa's story.

Helping a Neighbor

One afternoon last week, I was looking out of my window when I saw some thick black smoke. It was coming from my neighbor's kitchen. I ran to the house and banged on the back door. There was no answer! I was very worried, so I called 911.

The fire truck arrived five minutes later. The firefighters broke the kitchen window and put out the fire. I went around to the front of the house and there was my neighbor. He was doing some yard work. "Where's the fire?" he asked. "In your kitchen!" I replied.

Luckily, the fire wasn't serious, but the kitchen walls were black from the smoke. My neighbor said he will never try to cook and do yard work at the same time again.

WRITER'S NOTE
Add details to make your description more vivid. For example, "thick black smoke" gives us a picture of the smoke and makes the situation sound more dramatic.

D Check your understanding. Number the sentences in the correct order.

_____ The firefighters came to George's house.

_____ A fire started in George's kitchen.

_____ George went out to the front yard.

_____ George's neighbor called 911.

__1__ George was cooking his dinner.

3-38

E **Listen. Complete the forms.**

Emergency Report	Emergency Report	Emergency Report
Name: _Al Andrews_	Name: _Parvin Mulla_	Name: _Ella Chapman_
Emergency: _____	Emergency: _____	Emergency: _____
_____	_____	_____
Place: _____	Place: _____	Place: _____

3-38

F **Compare emergency reports with your partner. Listen again and check your work.**

2 Plan

A **Work with a partner. Imagine you saw a car accident, an explosion, or a flood. Ask and answer questions about the emergency.**

B **Answer the questions in your notebook. Use the information about your emergency from 2A.**

1. When? What? Where?
2. What did you see, hear, and feel? What did you do?
3. What happened next? What happened in the end?

3 Write

A **Write a story about the emergency from 2A. Use your notes from 2B.**

> An Emergency
>
> _____ , there was a _____ in _____ . I saw _____ and _____ . It was _____ .
> I was very _____ , so I called 911.
>
> The _____ arrived _____ later. They _____ and _____ . They _____ and _____ .
> In the end, _____ .
>
> Luckily, the _____ wasn't _____ , but the _____ were _____ . I decided that I will
> never _____ again.

B **Share your writing. Read your story to a partner.**

▸▸**TEST YOURSELF**

Complete the following sentences. Share your responses with your teacher.

1. After this writing lesson, I can…   2. I need more help with…

1 Explore the past continuous

A Look at the picture. Read the story about Ramiro. What are the people doing? What happened?

When I left home yesterday morning, it was raining very heavily. I was driving to work when I saw some police cars in front of me. A police officer was standing in the road, and he stopped my car. I wasn't driving very fast. The police officer told me to take another route because there was a flood.

B Analyze the sentences in 1A. Which verbs describe a past event that continued for some time? Which verbs describe a single short event?

C Study the grammar. Read the charts.

The past continuous					
Affirmative statements					
I	was		We		
You	were		You		
He She It	was	driving.	They	were	driving.

Negative statements					
I	wasn't		We		
You	weren't		You		
He She It	wasn't	driving.	They	weren't	driving.

SPELLING NOTE

make → making (e)
have → having (e)
sit → sitting
run → running

D Complete the sentences. Use the past continuous.

1. Julia _____ to work when she saw an accident. (drive)

2. When we left home, it _____ heavily. (not rain)

3. Marco _____ a coffee break when he heard an explosion. (have)

4. We _____ at our desks when the fire alarm went off. (not sit)

5. They _____ lunch when there was a sudden power outage. (eat)

2 Practice using the past continuous and the simple past

A Listen to the descriptions of the situations below. Mark the sentences
T (true) or *F* (false). Change the false sentences. Make them true.

3-39

Bob

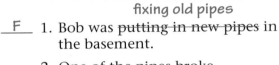

fixing old pipes

FIRE

Julie

_F_ 1. Bob was ~~putting in new pipes~~ in
the basement.

_____ 2. One of the pipes broke.

_____ 3. He turned off the electricity.

_____ 4. The water flooded the basement.

_____ 5. Julie and her co-workers were
having a coffee break.

_____ 6. They heard a fire engine.

_____ 7. They ran to the emergency exit.

_____ 8. They waited for the police.

B Look at the pictures in 2A. Complete the sentences.
Use the simple past or the past continuous.

1. Bob _____ pipes in the basement when a pipe _____ . He _____ off the
main water supply, so the water _____ the basement.

2. Julie and her co-workers _____ a staff meeting in the conference room
when the fire alarm _____ off. They _____ to the emergency exit
and _____ for the fire department.

C Talk to a partner. Follow the directions. Take turns.

Student A: Make true and false statements about the pictures in 2A.
Use simple past or past continuous.

Student B: Say: *That's true.* or *That's false.* Then correct the false statements.

A: *Bob was fixing the water supply.*

B: *That's false. He was fixing an old pipe.*

3 Practice using questions in the past

A Study the chart. Listen and repeat the questions.

	Information questions	Yes/no questions
Past continuous	What was he doing? What were they doing?	Was he fixing a pipe? Were they having a meeting?
Simple past	What did he do? What did they do?	Did he turn off the water supply? Did they call the fire department?

B Match the questions with the answers.

_____ 1. What happened to Nina?

_____ 2. What was she doing?

_____ 3. What happened to Elena and Viktor?

_____ 4. Were they driving to work?

a. They had an accident.

b. Yes, they were.

c. There was a fire in her kitchen.

d. She was baking cookies.

C Complete the conversations.

1. **A:** What happened at the factory?

   B: There was a gas explosion.

   A: Oh, no! What _____ they _____ when it happened?

   B: They were repairing the gas pipes.

   A: What _____ they _____ afterwards?

   B: They closed the factory for a week.

2. **A:** What happened at Samara's house?

   B: There was a flood in her basement.

   A: Oh, no! _____ she _____ the laundry at the time?

   B: Yes, she was.

   A: Where _____ she _____ afterwards?

   B: She went to stay with her parents.

4 Practice talking about an emergency

A Work in groups of three. Choose one situation from the box below. Tell your group about the emergency. Your group will ask questions for more details.

A: *Did you hear about Ben?*

B: *No. What happened to him?*

A: *He was driving on the highway when his car got stuck in the snow.*

C: *Oh, no! What did he do?*

> car stuck in a blizzard
> fire in a restaurant kitchen
> robbery in a store
> power outage after a hurricane

B Tell your group about an emergency that you experienced at work or at home. What happened? Did anyone help you? Your group will ask you questions for more details.

▶▶ **TEST YOURSELF**

Close your book. Tell a partner about a crime or an emergency that happened in the news this week or last week.

There was a fire on…

1 Listen to learn: making a 911 call

A Look at the video title and vocabulary with your classmates. Which words are new to you?

911 operator

medical emergency

WHEN TO CALL 911

B Listen. Is the 911 operator speaking? How do you know?
3-41

C Listen again. Which of these things are 911 emergencies?
3-41 Mark the emergencies *E*. Mark the non-emergencies *NE*.

1. Police
   - <u>NE</u> stolen bicycle
   - _____ a robbery

2. Fire
   - _____ a fire or smoke
   - _____ a cat in a tree

3. Medical
   - _____ a small cut or burn
   - _____ a broken leg

D Discuss this question with your classmates:

What are some other reasons to call 911?

2 Practice your pronunciation

A Listen and say the words. How many syllables are in each word?
3-42 Which syllable is stressed?

	Syllables	Stressed syllable
1. accident	3	first
2. important	3	second
3. information	4	third

NEED HELP?

Stressed syllables are a little louder and stronger than unstressed ones.

B Listen and say the words. How many syllables are there?
3-43 Put a dot (•) over the stressed syllable.

1. operator
2. ambulance
3. medication
4. emergency

3 Practice making an emergency call

A Listen and read the conversation. What information does the operator ask for?

3-44

Operator: 911. What's your emergency?

Man: There's a medical emergency. We need an ambulance right away.

Operator: Where are you?

Man: I'm at the intersection of Oakfield Road and Bridge Street.

Operator: What happened?

Man: There was an accident. A man was riding his bike and crashed into a tree.

Operator: Is he hurt?

Man: Yes, he is. I think he hit his head.

Operator: Stay on the phone and wait for instructions. Help is on the way.

B Listen and mark the answers to the questions.

3-45

1. a. Yes, there is. b. No, there isn't. 3. a. Yes, he is. b. No, he isn't.
2. a. Yes, there was. b. No, there wasn't. 4. a. Yes, he does. b. No, he doesn't.

C Think about the grammar. Look at the conversation and answer the questions.

1. How many *wh-* questions are there?
2. How many *yes/no* questions are there?

D Study the grammar. Practice the questions and answers with a partner.

There was / were	Was there...? / Were there...?
There was a robbery at the supermarket last week. **There wasn't** any smoke.	**Was there** a flood on the highway? Yes, there was. / No, there wasn't.
There were two explosions in a factory yesterday. **There weren't** any injuries.	**Were there** any injuries? Yes, there were. / No, there weren't.

E Work with a partner. Make new questions about the situation in 3A.

A: *Was there an accident?* **B:** *Yes, there was.*

152 Unit 11 Lesson 4

4 Make conversation: asking for help

A Work with a partner. Make a new conversation.

A: 911. What's your emergency?

B: There's a _____ . We need _____ right away.

A: Where are you?

B: I'm at _____ .

A: What happened?

B: There was a _____ .

A: Were there any injuries?

B: _____ .

A: Stay on the phone. Help is on the way.

B Present your conversation to another pair. Observe their conversation.

AT WORK ▸ Making an emergency call

 3-46

A Listen to the conversation. What is happening? Who is Karl talking to?

There's a problem in the delivery area.

OK, I'll take care of it. I'll send a plumber over there.

B Work with a partner. Take turns making an emergency call to your supervisor or manager in each situation.

Situation 1: You are on the highway driving a truck filled with frozen food, and the refrigeration isn't working.

Situation 2: You are working in a hotel kitchen, and there was a small fire in the grill. You are worried it may happen again.

▸▸ TEST YOURSELF

Act out this situation with a classmate. Take turns with each role.

Student: Describe an emergency situation that happened at school.
Teacher: Respond to the emergency.

1 Build reading strategies

A Read the definitions. Complete the sentences. Describe the picture.

evacuate: leave a place because it is dangerous

prepare: get ready for something

rescue: save someone from a dangerous situation

1. The firefighters helped _____ people from their flooded homes.

2. It's a good idea to _____ for an emergency before it happens.

3. Sometimes people have to _____ their homes during an emergency.

B Work with a partner. Check (✔) the things you do to prepare for an emergency.

☐ Listen to the news.

☐ Turn off the electricity.

☐ Find the emergency exit.

☐ Talk to your family.

☐ Read safety information.

☐ Prepare an emergency kit.

C Preview the website below. How many types of emergency are mentioned?

D Read the website. Why is it important to be ready for an emergency?

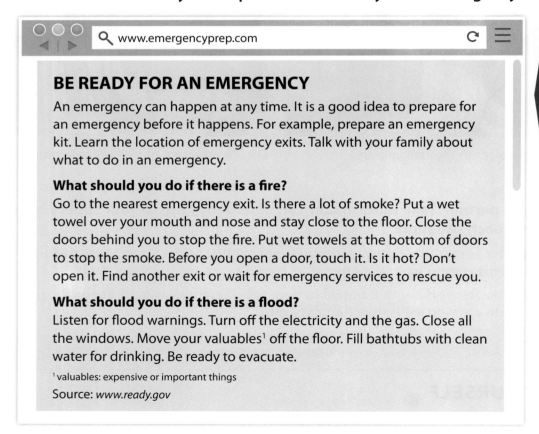

www.emergencyprep.com

BE READY FOR AN EMERGENCY

An emergency can happen at any time. It is a good idea to prepare for an emergency before it happens. For example, prepare an emergency kit. Learn the location of emergency exits. Talk with your family about what to do in an emergency.

What should you do if there is a fire?
Go to the nearest emergency exit. Is there a lot of smoke? Put a wet towel over your mouth and nose and stay close to the floor. Close the doors behind you to stop the fire. Put wet towels at the bottom of doors to stop the smoke. Before you open a door, touch it. Is it hot? Don't open it. Find another exit or wait for emergency services to rescue you.

What should you do if there is a flood?
Listen for flood warnings. Turn off the electricity and the gas. Close all the windows. Move your valuables[1] off the floor. Fill bathtubs with clean water for drinking. Be ready to evacuate.

[1] valuables: expensive or important things
Source: *www.ready.gov*

READER'S NOTE
Before you start reading an article, read the headings first. They can help you decide if this article is the one you need or not.

E Listen and read the article again. Which ideas were new for you?

3-47

F **Choose the correct words. Circle a or b.**

1. In a fire, you should _____ .
   a. turn off the electricity
   b. go to an emergency exit

2. In a fire, you should _____ .
   a. close doors
   b. fill sinks with clean water

3. In a flood, you should _____ .
   a. open the windows
   b. turn off the gas

4. In a flood, you should _____ .
   a. be ready to evacuate
   b. stay in your kitchen

G **Complete the sentences. Use the words in the box.**

evacuate	valuables	prepare	rescue

1. To be ready for an emergency, you should _____ an emergency kit.
2. In a flood, you should move your _____ upstairs.
3. In an emergency, you may have to _____ your home.
4. In a fire, you might have to wait for emergency services to _____ you.

2 Read an emergency kit checklist

A **Read the emergency kit checklist. Check (✔) the items you have at home.**

Emergency Kit Checklist

☐ food   ☐ water   ☐ blanket
☐ first-aid kit ☐ radio   ☐ flashlight
☐ knife   ☐ batteries   ☐ can opener

B **Think about it. Talk about the questions with your classmates.**

1. Why do you need the items in the checklist? What is each item for?

2. Add two of the items below to your emergency kit. Tell your partner why they are important.

newspaper	medicine	candy	hot water bottle	extra clothes

⏻ BRING IT TO LIFE

Choose an emergency that happens in your state, such as a hurricane. Find information on the Internet about the safety procedures for this emergency. Talk about the information with your class.

A Work with a team. Look at the picture. Ask and answer the questions.

1. What are these people doing?
2. What items are they packing?
3. When are these items necessary?
4. What other items are not included in the picture?
5. Choose one item in the picture. Why is it important to have this at home?
6. Which of these items do you have in your home or workplace?

B Work with a team. Write a conversation of 6–8 lines for the people in the picture. Decide what to put in your emergency kit.

A: What should we put into our emergency kit?

B: I think we should have a…because we can use it to…

C Share your emergency kit list with your class.

D Talk to your team. Tell your team about a situation when one of these items was very useful for you. Your team will ask you questions to get more details.

I was cooking dinner in the kitchen, and we had a power outage. It was very useful to have a flashlight because I needed to turn off the gas on the stove.

E Work with a team. What should you do in an emergency? Each team will choose an emergency below.

| an earthquake | a fire | a flood | a blizzard | a hurricane |

F Copy the chart in your notebooks. Then use the Internet or other resources to find out what to do in the emergency situation.

What should we do in _____ ?	
Before	
1.	
2.	
3.	
During	
1.	
2.	
3.	

G Talk about your ideas with your teammates. Agree on a list of steps to take in your emergency.

H Work with your team to create a poster or a booklet that explains the steps to take in your emergency. Present it to your class.

PROBLEM SOLVING

3-48

A Listen and read about Min.

It's a clear, sunny day, but Min heard a hurricane warning for her area on the news. Her husband is in Mexico for business, her kids are at school, and she doesn't have a car. Min's at home alone, and she's worried about her house.

B Work with your classmates. Answer the questions.

1. What is Min's problem?
2. What should Min do? Think of two or three solutions to her problem.

C Write a note to Min.

Dear Min,
Here's some advice about what to do in a hurricane. First you should...

UNIT

12 Take the Day Off

A LOOK AT
- Recreation and entertainment
- The superlative
- Asking for opinions

LESSON 1 VOCABULARY

1 Learn about recreational activities

A Show what you know. Circle the words you know. Which of these activities do you do?

1. go hiking
2. play softball
3. go biking
4. go fishing
5. go camping
6. go skating

April, Yosemite National Park

May, our backyard

August, Town Beach

September, Lake George

October, State Park Campground

December, City Ice Rink

B Listen and look at the pictures. Which member of the family is speaking?
3-49

C Listen and repeat the words from 1A.
3-50

D Write the vocabulary. Look at the picture. Complete the sentences.

1. Dina and her family like to __go camping__ in October.
2. They sometimes _____ in August.
3. The children like to _____ in April.
4. Dina and her daughter always _____ in December.
5. Pedro and his son usually _____ in September.
6. Pedro and the children always _____ in May.

E Ask and answer questions with a partner.

1. What outdoor activities do you and your family enjoy? When do you do them?
2. What outdoor recreational facilities are there in your town or state?

2 Talk about entertainment

A **Work together. Match the words with the picture.**

_____ action   <u>1</u> animation   _____ romance

_____ history   _____ horror   _____ science fiction

_____ biography   _____ mystery   _____ documentary

B **Listen and check your answers.**

3-51

C **Talk to a partner. Ask and answer the questions about the picture in 2A.**

1. What kind of book is _Lost in Love_? ___It's a romance.___

2. What is the title of the horror movie? _____

3. What is the title of the biography? _____

4. What kind of book is _The Stolen Diamond_? _____

5. What is the title of the science fiction book? _____

6. What kind of book is _Ancient Rome_? _____

D **Think about it. Ask and answer the questions with your classmates.**

1. What do you like to do in your free time?

2. What other types of books and movies do you know?

▶▶**TEST YOURSELF**

Copy the chart in your notebook. Write the words from this lesson in the chart.

	Recreational activities	Entertainment
I enjoy…		
I don't enjoy…		
I don't know…		

1 Prepare to write

A Look at the list of weekend activities in 1B. Which things do you like to do?

B Look at the pictures. Listen to Dina's email. Check (✓) what Dina's family will do.

3-52

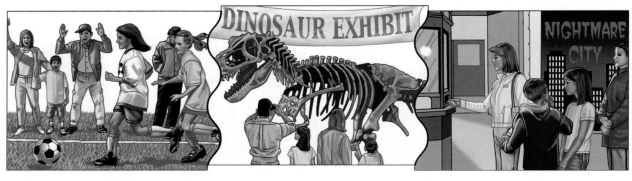

☐ go to the movies ☐ go to a soccer game ☐ listen to music
☐ go shopping ☐ go to the zoo ☐ go to a museum

C Listen again and read the email.

3-52

Subject: Weekend plans

Dear Lucinda,

   This weekend is a three-day weekend. It's going to be fun to spend time with my family. On Saturday, my daughter Gabriela is going to play in a soccer game with her school team, and we are all going to watch. Pedro and I like to talk with the other parents.

   On Sunday, we're going to visit the Science Museum. There is a new exhibit about dinosaurs. Sunday is the cheapest day to go to the museum because it's Family Day. We can buy one special ticket for the whole family for just $35.

   On Monday, we're going to go to the movies. Pedro and the children want to see a horror movie.

   Write soon and tell me about your plans for this weekend.
Dina

WRITER'S NOTE

After introducing the main idea of a paragraph, include some supporting details. For example, in paragraph 2, the main idea is about visiting the science museum. The supporting detail is about the dinosaur exhibit.

D Check your understanding. Mark the sentences *T* (true) or *F* (false).

_____ 1. Dina is going to stay home this weekend.

_____ 2. Gabriela is going to play soccer.

_____ 3. Dina and her family can visit the museum on Sunday for free.

_____ 4. They're going to see a movie about dinosaurs.

E **Listen and complete the sentences.**

3-53

1. Maria is going to _____ on _____ .
2. Jason is going to _____ with _____ .
3. Maria and Jason are going to _____ .
   They are going to _____ .

F **Compare sentences with your partner.**
Listen again and check your work.

3-53

THIS WEEKEND

YOGA: Saturday 7–8:30 a.m. at Green National Park. Relaxation in a natural setting. Free.

FAMILY FUN BIKE RIDE: Saturday 9:30 a.m. at Town Beach Clubhouse

COUNTRY MUSIC CONCERT: Sunday 2–5 p.m. at Waterside Park. Bring a picnic!

---

2 Plan

A **Complete the chart with information about your plans for this weekend.**

	morning	afternoon	evening
Saturday			
Sunday			

B **Talk with a partner. Ask and answer questions about your plans.**
Then add more details to your charts.

Where are you going to go on Saturday morning? Who are you going to go with?
What are you going to do?

3 Write

A **Write an email about your plans. Use your ideas from 2A. Give your email a subject line.**

> ○ ○ ○
>
> To: _____
> Subject: _____
>
> Dear _____ ,
>   On Saturday, I'm going to _____
> _____
>   On Sunday we're going to _____
> _____

B **Share your writing. Read your email to a partner.**

▶▶ TEST YOURSELF

Complete the following sentences. Share your responses with your teacher.

1. After this writing lesson, I can…
2. I need more help with…

1 Explore the superlative

A Look at the pictures. Read the movie descriptions. What type of movie is each one? Which movies would you like to see?

B Analyze the sentences in 1A. Underline the adjectives in the movie descriptions. Which adjective is different from the others?

C Study the grammar. Read the chart. Which type of adjective uses *most*?

The superlative			
	Adjective	**Superlative**	**Notes**
One syllable	long large sad	the longest the largest the saddest	Add *-est* or *-st*. For words like *sad*, double the final consonant.
Ending in *-y*	funny scary	the funniest the scariest	Change *y* to *i* and add *-est*.
Two or more syllables	exciting famous	the most exciting the most famous	Put *the most* in front of the adjective.
Irregular forms	good bad	the best the worst	

D Complete the sentences. Use the superlative of the adjectives in parentheses.

1. *Goodbye for Now* was <u>the saddest</u> movie this year. (sad)

2. *Monsters 2* was definitely _____ movie this year. (bad)

3. *Nightmare City* was _____ movie this year. (scary)

4. Paul Knight was _____ actor in *Distant Star*. (famous)

5. What was _____ movie this year? (good)

E Work with a partner. Match the sentences in 1D with the rules in 1C.

2 Practice questions with the superlative

A Complete the questions about Ben's list. Use the superlative form of the adjectives in the advertisement.

Ben's List of "The Most" and "The Best" in the U.S.

Popular tourist destination: The Grand Canyon
Expensive hotel: In Las Vegas
Scary sport: Zip-lining
Cheap vacation: Camping

1. What is _the most popular_ tourist destination according to Ben's List?

2. Where is _____ hotel in the U.S.?

3. What is _____ sport in the U.S.?

4. What is _____ type of vacation in the U.S.?

B Answer the questions. Use the information in 2A.

According to Ben's list, ...

1. _the most popular tourist destination in the U.S. is the Grand Canyon._

2. _____

3. _____

4. _____

3 Practice using the comparative and the superlative

🔊 3-54 **A** Listen to these fitness instructors comparing activities. Complete the sentences with the comparative or superlative form of the adjectives in the box.

| convenient | exciting | friendly | relaxing | healthy |

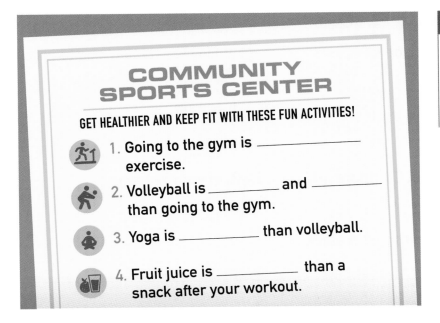

COMMUNITY SPORTS CENTER

GET HEALTHIER AND KEEP FIT WITH THESE FUN ACTIVITIES!

1. Going to the gym is _____ exercise.

2. Volleyball is _____ and _____ than going to the gym.

3. Yoga is _____ than volleyball.

4. Fruit juice is _____ than a snack after your workout.

> **GRAMMAR NOTE**
>
> **Comparative and superlative**
> Use the comparative to talk about two things.
> Use the superlative to talk about three or more things.

B Talk with a partner. Say if you agree or disagree with the sentences in 3A.

C Work in a group of four people. Complete the chart with your group's opinions.

A: *Which sport is the healthiest?*

B: *I think swimming is the healthiest sport.*

C: *I disagree. I think running is healthier than swimming.*

Which sport is...?	
(healthy) the healthiest	
(dangerous)	
(relaxing)	
(boring)	
(cheap)	
(expensive)	

D Talk about the answers in the chart with your class.

4 Answer a questionnaire about free-time activities

A Read the questionnaire. Circle your answers.

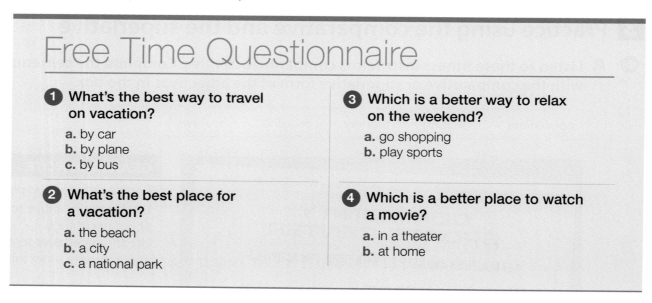

Free Time Questionnaire

1 What's the best way to travel on vacation?
  a. by car
  b. by plane
  c. by bus

2 What's the best place for a vacation?
  a. the beach
  b. a city
  c. a national park

3 Which is a better way to relax on the weekend?
  a. go shopping
  b. play sports

4 Which is a better place to watch a movie?
  a. in a theater
  b. at home

B Work in a group of three. Compare answers. Explain your reasons.

I think the best way to travel is by car because it is the most convenient.

C Talk about the answers with your class.

▶▶ TEST YOURSELF

Close your book. Use your notebook. Write six sentences about your opinions of free-time activities. Which activity is the most exciting? The scariest? The most boring?

1 Listen to learn: expressing opinions

A Look at the pictures. Which things do you do most often? Number them from 1 (often) to 4 (not very often).

_____ watch sports _____ watch a TV show _____ go to a concert _____ eat out

B 3-55 Listen to the three conversations. What is the main topic of each conversation?

C 3-55 Listen again. Complete the chart.

Questions	Conversation 1	Conversation 2	Conversation 3
Main topic of conversation			
Did the man like it? Yes or no?			
Did the woman like it? Yes or no?			

2 Practice your pronunciation

A 3-56 Listen. Circle the stressed syllable in each word. Then listen again and repeat.

amazing	fantastic	horrible	incredible	awesome	terrible

B 3-57 Listen. Notice the difference between the two replies. We can use stronger syllable stress to show that we really liked or disliked something.

A: How was the game last night?

B: It was amazing. (It was good.) / It was amazing! (It was really good.)

C 3-58 Listen and check (✓) whether the speaker expresses a normal opinion or a strong opinion.

	Normal [*]	Strong [***]
1. The movie was fantastic.	☐	☐
2. The food was delicious.	☐	☐
3. The game was awesome.	☐	☐
4. The concert was terrible.	☐	☐

3 Practice asking for and giving opinions

 A Listen and read the conversation. Do they agree or disagree?

3-59

Sheryl: How was the baseball game last night?

Brian: It was great! Pete Vargas was playing. I think he's the best player on the team.

Sheryl: I think so too!

Brian: What did you do last night?

Sheryl: I watched a sci-fi show on TV—*New Planet*.

Brian: What did you think of it?

Sheryl: I don't think it's very good. The show was better last season.

Brian: Really? I heard it was quite good.

B Think about the grammar. Look at the conversation and answer the questions.

1. What are two ways of asking for an opinion?

2. What is one way to agree? What is one way to disagree?

C Study the grammar. Listen and repeat the questions and answers in the chart.

3-60

Say your opinion	Agree	Disagree
I think this movie is fantastic!	So do I. I think so, too. Me too.	Really? I don't think so. I think it's terrible.
I don't think this TV show is very good.	Neither do I. I don't either. Me neither.	Really? I think it's great.

D Work with a partner. Take turns expressing an opinion. Then agree or disagree with your partner.

Student A:

I think Indian food is delicious.

I think horror movies are boring.

I don't think ice skating is difficult.

Student B:

I think Japanese food is fantastic.

I think action movies are exciting.

I don't think camping is very relaxing.

NEED HELP?

exciting

interesting

amazing

so-so

not bad

boring

Make conversation: agreeing and disagreeing with opinions

A Work with a partner. Make a new conversation.

A: How was the _____ yesterday?

B: It was great! I think _____ .

A: _____ . What did you do last night?

B: I _____ .

B: Really? What did you think of it?

A: I don't think _____ . _____ .

B: Really? _____ .

NEED HELP?

Ask for opinions
How was...?
What did you think of...?
Did you like...?

B Present your conversation to another pair. Observe their conversation.

AT WORK ⟩ Asking for opinions

A Listen to ways to ask for opinions.

3-61

How was the conference?

Did you like the presentation?

What did you think of the plans?

B Listen again. What are the speakers' opinions? Did they express a strong opinion?

3-61

1. __It was fantastic. (strong opinion)__

2. _____

3. _____

C Work with a partner. Practice the conversations above. Then ask your partner for his or her opinion about something new in your classroom or in your school. Agree or disagree.

▶TEST YOURSELF

Act out this situation with a classmate. Take turns with each role.

Worker A: You and your co-workers watched a staff training video this morning. Give your opinion of the video and ask your co-worker's opinion.

Worker B: Agree or disagree. Give a reason.

1 Build reading strategies

A Read the definitions. Use the words to describe the pictures.

border: the line between two countries, states, or cities

canyon: a valley with tall steep sides, often with a river at the bottom

sight: a famous or interesting place

view: what you can see from a certain place

B Preview the reading. What kind of magazine do you think this article is from?

C Read the article. Where are these places located?

Top Sights in the U.S.

Washington, D.C., is the capital[1] of the United States. One important building in Washington, D.C., is the White House. It is at 1600 Pennsylvania Avenue. The president lives and works there. Tours are available for the public and are free of charge. You need to write to your U.S. representative or senator for tickets at least three weeks in advance.

Niagara Falls is on the border between the United States and Canada. The two waterfalls that make up Niagara Falls are the largest waterfalls in North America. More than 750,000 gallons of water go over the falls each second. A boat called the Maid of the Mist takes tourists to the bottom of the falls.

The Grand Canyon is a large national park in Arizona. It is one of the most amazing places in the world. The canyon is 277 miles long and over one mile deep. Its natural beauty brings more than five million visitors to this park every year. Visitors can go hiking, camping, or birdwatching. Or they can just stand and enjoy the view!

The Golden Gate Bridge is in San Francisco on the West Coast of the United States. The bridge is the most famous sight in San Francisco. It opened in 1937 and is 1.7 miles long. From the bridge, pedestrians, cyclists, and car drivers can enjoy the view of the Pacific Ocean and San Francisco Bay.

[1]capital: city where the government of a country or state is located

READER'S NOTE

Identify the words that can help you find the location of these places on a map. Try to visualize locations on a map as you read this article.

ACADEMIC

 D Listen and read the article again. Which place do you want to visit the most?

3-62

E Mark the sentences *T* (true) or *F* (false).

_____ 1. Visitors can go to the White House at any time.

_____ 2. The largest waterfalls in North America are the Niagara Falls.

_____ 3. Grand Canyon National Park is in Arizona.

_____ 4. You can walk or drive across the Golden Gate Bridge.

_____ 5. You can see the Atlantic Ocean from the Golden Gate Bridge.

F Complete the sentences. Use the words in the box.

sight	view	border	capital

1. Washington, D.C., is the _____ of the United States.

2. You can get a good _____ of Niagara Falls from a boat.

3. Niagara Falls is on the _____ between the U.S. and Canada.

4. The Golden Gate Bridge is the most famous _____ in San Francisco.

2 Read a map

A Look at the map. Write the places from the article on the map.

NEED HELP?

in the Northeast

on the West Coast

in the Midwest

on the border

B Ask and answer questions about the location of each place. Use the map in 2A and the information in the article in 1C.

C Think about it. Talk about these questions with a partner.

1. Name three more famous sights in the U.S. Mark them on your map.

2. Plan a journey together to visit all these places and decide in what order you will visit each place. Draw the route on the map.

⏻ BRING IT TO LIFE

Find information on the Internet about the most popular tourist destinations in the U.S. Choose two places to visit. What famous sights are there? Talk about them with your classmates.

TEAMWORK & LANGUAGE REVIEW

A Work with a team. Look at the picture. Ask and answer the questions.

1. What are these people doing?
2. How do they feel?
3. What equipment do you need for these activities?
4. Which of the activities are easy?
5. Which of the activities are dangerous?
6. Which activities do you like?
7. Which activities do you want to try?
8. How are the activities good for your health?

B Work with a team. Write a conversation of 6–8 lines for two of the people in the picture. Share your conversation with your classmates.

A: I think hiking is the best way to relax on the weekend. What do you think?
B: I think so, too!

C Complete the sentences with the comparative or superlative form of the words in parentheses.

1. Action movies are _____ than romance movies. (interesting)
2. Hiking is _____ than fishing. (relaxing)
3. Skating is _____ than biking. (easy)
4. I think horror movies are _____ type of movie in the U.S. (popular)
5. I think running is _____ sport. (healthy)

D Take turns reading each sentence in C to your team. Say if you agree or disagree with each statement and why.

E Work with your team. Choose one of the topics below. Interview all the students in the class and write down their answers. Ask them to give reasons for their answers and take notes.

Topic 1: What is the most popular sport that people in the class play or do?

Topic 2: What is the most popular sport that people in the class like to watch?

Topic 3: What is the most popular type of TV show people in the class watch?

Topic 4: What is the most popular outdoor activity that people in the class do?

Topic 5: What is the most popular type of movie that people in the class watch?

A: *Stacy, what is your favorite sport?*

B: *I love volleyball.*

A: *Why do you like it?*

F Combine the data and discuss your findings.

G Write a summary.

> Our group found that the most popular _____ in this class is _____ . We found that _____ people like _____ , but only _____ people like _____ . Most people think that _____ is better than _____ . Nobody likes _____ . We think the reason for this is _____ .

H Talk about the results of your survey with your class.

PROBLEM SOLVING AT HOME

A Listen and read about Tara.

3-63

> Tara's children like to watch TV for four or more hours every day. Tara thinks TV is OK, but only for an hour each day. She thinks that there are better things for her children to do. When she tells her children that they should do other things, they say, "TV is more interesting than that." When she turns off the TV, her children get angry. Tara is worried about her children, but she doesn't know what to do.

B Work with your classmates. Answer the questions.

1. What is Tara's problem?

2. What can Tara do? Think of two or three solutions to her problem.

C Role-play a conversation between Tara and a friend. Present your role-play to the class.

A: *What's the matter, Tara?*

B: *It's my children. They watch too much TV!*

The simple present with *want to, like to, need to*

Affirmative statements

I You	want like need	
He She It	wants likes needs	to eat.
We You They	want like need	

Negative statements

I You	don't	want like need	
He She It	doesn't	want like need	to eat.
We You They	don't	want like need	

Contractions

do not = don't
does not = doesn't

Yes/No questions

Do	I you		
Does	he she it	want like need	to eat?
Do	we you they		

Short answers

Yes,	I you	do.	No,	I you	don't.
	he she it	does.		he she it	doesn't.
	we you they	do.		we you they	don't.

Information questions

What	do	I you	want	to study?
Who	does	he she	like	to visit?
How	does	it	like	to eat?
Where When Why	do	we you they	need	to work?

The future with *will*

Affirmative statements

I You He She It We You They	will	work.

Negative statements

I You He She It We You They	won't	eat.

Contractions

I will = I'll
you will = you'll
he will = he'll
she will = she'll
it will = it'll
we will = we'll
they will = they'll

will not = won't

Yes/No questions

Will	I you	
	he she it	work?
	we you they	

Short answers

Yes,	I you	will.	No,	I you	won't.
	he she it			he she it	
	we you they			we you they	

Information questions

What	will	I you	study?
Who	will	he she	see?
How	will	it	work?
Where When Why	will	we you they	work?

The simple past

Affirmative statements		
I You He She It We You They	liked	the food.

Negative statements			
I You He She It We You They	didn't	like	the food.

Contractions
did not = didn't

Yes/No questions			
Did	I you he she it we you they	like	the food?

Short answers						
Yes,	I you he she it we you they	did.	No,	I you he she it we you they	didn't.

Information questions			
What How	did	I you	do?
Who	did	he she it	see?
Where When Why	did	we you they	go?

Past tense of irregular verbs				
be—was/were	drink—drank	hear—heard	put—put	spend—spent
become—became	drive—drove	hit—hit	read—read	stand—stood
break—broke	eat—ate	hurt—hurt	ride—rode	steal—stole
bring—brought	fall—fell	keep—kept	ring—rang	take—took
buy—bought	feed—fed	know—knew	run—ran	tell—told
catch—caught	feel—felt	leave—left	say—said	think—thought
choose—chose	find—found	lend—lent	see—saw	throw—threw
come—came	forget—forgot	let—let	sell—sold	understand—understood
cost—cost	get—got	lose—lost	send—sent	wake up—woke up
cut—cut	give—gave	make—made	sit—sat	wear—wore
do—did	go—went	meet—met	sleep—slept	withdraw—withdrew
draw—drew	have—had	pay—paid	speak—spoke	write—wrote

Purpose and reasons with *to* and *because*

Purpose with *to* + verb		
Carol used her English book	to study	the new vocabulary.
		grammar charts.

Reasons with *because*		
Kathryn withdrew twenty dollars	because	her son needs money.
		she wants to buy a book.
		she needed money.
		she wanted to eat lunch.

The past continuous

Affirmative statements

I	was	
You	were	
He She It	was	walking.
We You They	were	

Negative statements

I	wasn't	
You	weren't	
He She It	wasn't	walking.
We You They	weren't	

Contractions

was not = wasn't
were not = weren't

Yes/No questions

Was	I	
Were	you	
Was	he she it	walking?
Were	we you they	

Short answers

Yes,	I	was.	No,	I	wasn't.
	you	were.		you	weren't.
	he she it	was.		he she it	wasn't.
	we you they	were.		we you they	weren't.

Information questions

Where	was	I	working last year?
Why	were	you	eating cake?
Who	was	he she	visiting?
When	was	it	raining?
What How	were	we you they	doing yesterday?

Past continuous		Simple past
He was studying	when	the teacher spoke.
They were sleeping		the phone rang.

Polite statements and requests

Affirmative statements

I You He She It We You They	would like	to help. a refund.

Negative statements

I You He She It We You They	wouldn't like	to help. a refund.

Questions

May Can Could	I you he she it we	help, please?
Would	you they	like to help?

Short answers

Yes,	I you he she it we you they	may. can. would.	No,	I you he she it we you they	may not. can't. wouldn't.

... have to

	might must should	sleep.
one It		
We You They		

Negative statements

I You		
He She It	might not must not should not	sleep.
We You They		

Contractions

In the U.S., people usually don't make negative contractions with *might* or *must*. However, you can use contractions with *should not*: *shouldn't*.

Notes

For things that are possible, use *might*.
For things that are necessary, use *must*.
For things that are advisable, use *should*.

Yes/No questions

Do	I you		
Does	he she it	have to	sleep?
Do	we you they		

Notes

In the U.S., people usually don't ask questions with *might* or *must*.
~~Might she sleep?~~
~~Must she sleep?~~
However, we can make questions with *should*.
    Should I go to the doctor?

Short answers

	I you	do.		I you	don't.
Yes,	he she it	does.	No,	he she it	doesn't.
	we you they	do.		we you they	don't.

Information questions with *have to*

How often		make photocopies?
How many photocopies	does he have to	make?

Prepositions

Prepositions of time		Notes
I was a student	in 2001.	Use *in* for years and months.
	in August.	
The class begins	on Monday.	Use *on* for days and dates.
	on July 24th.	
The movie starts	at 10:45.	Use *at* for times.
	at two o'clock.	
January is	before February.	
December is	after November.	

e and superlative

	Adjective	Comparative	Superlative	
...able	small nice hot	smaller nicer hotter	the smallest the nicest the hottest	... fir...
Ending in -y	happy noisy	happier noisier	the happiest the noisiest	For c... and a... For sup... and add...
Two or more syllables	famous expensive comfortable	more famous more expensive more comfortable	the most famous the most expensive the most comfortable	For compar... ...n front of adjec... For superlative, add *most* in front of adjectives.
Irregular forms	good bad far	better worse farther	the best the worst the farthest	

Comparatives in sentences				Notes
The computer is	cheaper noisier more expensive better	than	the photocopier.	Use the comparative to talk about two things.

Superlatives in sentences			Notes
This computer is	(one of) the cheapest (one of) the most popular	of all. in the store. this week.	Use the superlative to talk about groups of three or more things.

Questions with *which*		Answers
Which is bigger,	a house or a factory?	A factory is.
Which building is bigger,		A factory is bigger.

Adverbs of degree: *much, a lot, a little, a bit*					
A laptop	is	a little/a bit	more expensive	than	a tablet.
A used car		much/a lot	cheaper		a new car.

Adjectives with *too* and *not…enough*

Too + adjective			Notes
It's They're	too	small. noisy. expensive.	*too* = more than is good Use *too* + adjective.

Not…enough				Notes
It's They're	not	big quiet cheap	enough.	*enough* = the right amount It's not cheap enough. = It's too expensive.

...tive statements	
...s	a cookie.
	an egg.

Singular negative statements	
We don't have	a cookie.
There isn't	an egg.

Plural affirmative statements	
We have	two cookies.
There are	three eggs.

Plural negative statements	
We don't have	any cookies.
There aren't	any eggs.

Singular questions	
Do you have	a cookie?
	an egg?

Answers
Yes, we have a cookie.
No, we don't have an egg.

Plural questions		
Do you have	any	cookies?
		eggs?

Answers
Yes, we have some cookies.
No, we don't have any eggs.

Questions with *how many*		
How many	cookies eggs potatoes vegetables carrots	are there?

Answers	
There is	one cookie. one egg.
There are	many potatoes. a lot of vegetables. a few carrots.

Noncount nouns

Affirmative statements	
We have	some soup. two cans of soup.
There is	some soup.
There are	two cans of soup.

Negative statements	
We don't have	any soup. much soup.
There isn't	

Questions with *how much*		
How much	soup ice cream coffee spaghetti	is there?

Answers	
There is	one can of soup.
There are	two cartons of ice cream.
There is	a lot of coffee. a little spaghetti.

Direct and indirect objects

	Direct object	Indirect object	Notes
I'll give	the message	to him.	Some verbs, such as *give*, *send*, *show*, and *write*, can have two objects. When the indirect object follows the direct object, we use the prepositions *to* or *for*.
	Indirect object	**Direct object**	
I'll give	him	the message.	

...USA

...Street, Oxford, OX2 6DR, United Kingdom

...University Press is a department of the University of Oxford.
...the University's objective of excellence in research, scholarship,
...ucation by publishing worldwide. Oxford is a registered trade
...rk of Oxford University Press in the UK and in certain other countries

© Oxford University Press 2017

The moral rights of the author have been asserted

First published in 2017

2021 2020 2019

10 9 8 7 6

No unauthorized photocopying

ISBN: 9 78 0 19 449377 2 STUDENT BOOK (PACK)

ISBN: 9 78 0 19 449302 4 STUDENT BOOK (PACK COMPONENT)

ISBN: 9 78 0 19 440479 2 OEVT APP

Printed in China

This book is printed on paper from certified and well-managed sources

ACKNOWLEDGMENTS

Back cover photograph: Oxford University Press building/David Fisher

Illustrations by: Cover, Jeff Mangiat / Mendola Artist Representatives. 5W
Infographics, p. 14, p. 19, p. 22, p. 31, p. 40, p. 56, p. 74, p. 87, p. 99, p. 104
(middle), p. 109 (right), p. 112, p. 122, p. 130, p. 136, p. 137, p. 161, p. 163
(bottom), p. 164, p. 169; Kenneth Batelmann, p. 88, p. 117, p. 131; Annie
Bissett p. 135 (bus rules), p. 145; Dan Brown, p. 47, p. 103; Mark Collins p. 134;
Lyndall Culbertson p. 81, p. 92, p. 123 (realia), p. 147; Ken Dewar p. 89, p. 90
(food), p. 112 (first-aid kit), p. 155; Bill Dickson, p. 132, p. 146; Jody Emery p.
25, p. 26; Mike Gardner, p. 4, p. 6, p. 34, p. 58, p. 88, p. 104 (top), p. 114, p. 116,
p. 155, p. 162; Garth Glazier/AA Reps p. 115; John Goodwin, p. 8, p. 12, p. 26,
p. 109 (left), p. 149; Glenn Gustafson p. 128; Peter Hoey, p. 21, p. 23, p. 29, p.
85, p. 108, p. 113, p. 127, p. 157; Stewart Holmes/Illustration Ltd., p. 72; Mike
Hortens p. 36; Rod Hunt p. 33; Janos Jantner, p. 5, p. 20, p. 75; Ken Joudrey/
Munro Campagna p. 44; Uldis Klavins p. 19, p. 95; John Kurtz, p. 13, p. 17, p.
27, p. 55, p. 68, p. 111, p. 124, p. 130, p. 138; Jeffrey Lindberg p. 80; Deb Lofaso,
p. 10 (middle), p. 28, p. 37, p. 43, p. 70, p. 98, p. 123, p. 140, p. 163 (top), p.
168; Rose Lowry p. 140; Karen Minot p. 46 (realia), p. 60 (realia), p. 116, p. 162;
Peter Miserendino/P.T. Pie Illustrations p. 86; Jay Montgomery p. 11, p. 123
(people); Derek Mueller p. 4, p. 158, p. 160; Tom Newsom p. 46 (woman), p. 50;
Geo Parkin, p. 18, p. 76, p. 96, p. 97, p. 120, p. 152, p. 153, p. 159, p. 166; Terry
Paczko p. 32, p. 102; Karen Pritchett p. 106; Mark Riedy/Scott Hull Associates
p. 142; Aaron Sacco, p. xiii, p. 10 (top), p. 64, p. 110, p. 151; Martin Sanders, p.
38, p. 61; Jeff Sanson/Schumann & Co., p. 30; Jane Spencer p. 6, p. 34, p. 48, p.
62, p. 148; Reed Sprunger/Jae Wagoner Artists Rep., p. 170; Eric Velasquez p.
144; Brad Walker p. 156; Simon Williams/Illustration Ltd., p. 16, p. 100.

*We would also like to thank the following for permission to reproduce the following
photographs*: Click Bestsellers / Shutterstock.com, Cover; simonkr/Getty
Images, ...Getty Ima... p. 14 (gradu... Alamy Stock ... p. 22 (brunette... mimagephotogr... Images/Alamy Sto... p. 41 (co-workers); Ja... PeopleImages/Getty I... Stock Photo, p. 53 (mai... 53 (accountant); Ariel Ske... Hill Street Studios/Getty In... Stock Photo, p. 65 (hard hat ... (face mask sign); Wittybear/Sh... Cotton/Alamy Stock Photo, p. 6... Alamy Stock Photo, p. 65 (apron s... 66 (spilled watermelons); Westend... l i g h t p o e t/Shutterstock.com, p. 6... Images, p. 67 (forklift); Fuse/Getty Ima... Shutterstock.com, p. 67 (power tools); S... (typing letter); leungchopan/Shutterstock... Solloway/Alamy Stock Photo, p. 67 (office clerk); Andy Dean Photography/
Shutterstock.com, p. 67 (man); imtmphoto/Shutterstock.com, p. 69
(businessmen); michaeljung/Shutterstock.com, p. 69 (supermarket workers);
Juice Images/Alamy Stock Photo, p. 69 (factory workers); David Lees/Getty
Images, p. 70 (business people shaking hands); Panther Media GmbH/Alamy
Stock Photo, p. 73 (businesswoman); Jose Luis Pelaez Inc/Getty Images, p. 74
(paying bills); Lars Zahner/Alamy Stock Photo, p. 78 (woman jogging); Kzenon/
Shutterstock.com, p. 78 (man eating dinner); Jacob Lund/Shutterstock.com,
p. 82 (woman working); pink_cotton_candy/Getty Images, p. 82 (sick man);
Pressmaster/Shutterstock.com, p. 83 (office meeting); asiseeit/Getty Images,
p. 83 (restaurant manager); wavebreakmedia/Shutterstock.com, p. 84 (senior
volunteers); Bikeworldtravel/Shutterstock.com, p. 90 (woman); Blend Images/
Shutterstock.com, p. 92 (woman); EM Arts/Shutterstock.com, p. 95 (grapes);
Sheila Fitzgerald/Shutterstock.com, p. 95 (soup); Leonid Nyshko/Alamy
Stock Photo, p. 95 (yogurt); Lost Mountain Studio/Shutterstock.com, p. 95
(sausages); Tischenko Irina/Shutterstock.com, p. 98 (fruits & vegetables);
stevecoleimages/Getty Images, p. 102 (pharmacist); wavebreakmedia/
Shutterstock.com, p. 104 (x-ray); Lawrence Gibbens/Alamy Stock Photo, p. 107
(boy fallen off bike); Art Directors & TRIP/Alamy Stock Photo, p. 107 (woman
burned hand); Ljupco/Getty Images, p. 107 (stomachache); Andrey_Popov/
Shutterstock.com, p. 107 (sprained ankle); pcruciatti/Shutterstock.com, p.
118 (Apple store); Monkey Business Images/Shutterstock.com, p. 118 (man
on laptop); guruXOX/Shutterstock.com, p. 121 (woman using ATM); olaser/
Getty Images, p. 121 (man buying suit); Rawpixel.com/Shutterstock.com, p.
121 (online shopping); shooarts/Shutterstock.com, p. 123 (sweater); Evikka/
Shutterstock.com, p. 123 (socks); Mega Pixel/Shutterstock.com, p. 123 (tie);
MilanMarkovic/Getty Images, p. 125 (doctor's office receptionist); Alistair
Berg/Getty Images, p. 125 (hotel receptionist); Studio51/Alamy Stock Photo,
p. 126 (wallet); Tom Grundy/Alamy Stock Photo, p. 135 (no parking sign);
Michael Burrell/Alamy Stock Photo, p. 135 (no smoking sign); gmstockstudio/
Shutterstock.com, p. 135 (no left turn sign); jojoo64/Getty Images, p. 135 (no
right turn sign); Sergio Azenha/Alamy Stock Photo, p. 137 (brunette woman);
Klaus Tiedge/Getty Images, p. 137 (Hispanic man); mimagephotography/
Shutterstock.com, p. 137 (African-American man); PacoRomero/Getty Images,
p. 137 (Asian woman); Monty Rakusen/Getty Images, p. 139 (security guard);
Yongyuan Dai/Getty Images, p. 139 (bank teller); Creatas/Getty Images, p. 139
(airport security); Jim Young/Reuters, p. 140 (Sonia Sotomayor); Jeff Morgan
16/Alamy Stock Photo, p. 154 (flooding); Justin Lewis/Getty Images, p. 163
(zip-lining); Jose Luis Pelaez/Getty Images, p. 165 (man watching TV); Daniel
Allan/Getty Images, p. 165 (woman watching TV); davide piras/Alamy Stock
Photo, p. 165 (band concert); Greatstock/Alamy Stock Photo, p. 165 (coffee
shop); Juice Images Ltd/Getty Images, p. 167 (business conference); Jose Luis
Pelaez Inc/Getty Images, p. 167 (doctors); bikeriderlondon/Shutterstock.com,
p. 167 (engineers); Bo Zaunders/Getty Images, p. 168 (White House); lastdjedai/
Shutterstock.com, p. 168 (Niagara Falls); Alan Majchrowicz/Getty Images, p.
168 (Grand Canyon); dibrova/Shutterstock.com, p. 168 (San Francisco).

Might, must, should, and have to

Affirmative statements

I You		
He She It	might must should	sleep.
We You They		

Negative statements

I You		
He She It	might not must not should not	sleep.
We You They		

Contractions

In the U.S., people usually don't make negative contractions with *might* or *must*. However, you can use contractions with *should not*: *shouldn't*.

Notes

For things that are possible, use *might*.
For things that are necessary, use *must*.
For things that are advisable, use *should*.

Yes/No questions

Do	I you		
Does	he she it	have to	sleep?
Do	we you they		

Notes

In the U.S., people usually don't ask questions with *might* or *must*.
~~Might she sleep?~~
~~Must she sleep?~~
However, we can make questions with *should*.
Should I go to the doctor?

Short answers

Yes,	I you	do.	No,	I you	don't.
	he she it	does.		he she it	doesn't.
	we you they	do.		we you they	don't.

Information questions with have to

How often	does he have to	make photocopies?
How many photocopies		make?

Prepositions

Prepositions of time		Notes
I was a student	in 2001.	Use *in* for years and months.
	in August.	
The class begins	on Monday.	Use *on* for days and dates.
	on July 24th.	
The movie starts	at 10:45.	Use *at* for times.
	at two o'clock.	
January is	before February.	
December is	after November.	

The comparative and superlative

	Adjective	Comparative	Superlative	Notes
One syllable	small nice hot	smaller nicer hotter	the smallest the nicest the hottest	For comparative, add -er or -r. For superlative, add -est or -st. For words like *hot*, double the final consonant.
Ending in -y	happy noisy	happier noisier	the happiest the noisiest	For comparative, change y to i and add -er. For superlative, change y to i and add -est.
Two or more syllables	famous expensive comfortable	more famous more expensive more comfortable	the most famous the most expensive the most comfortable	For comparative, add *more* in front of adjectives. For superlative, add *most* in front of adjectives.
Irregular forms	good bad far	better worse farther	the best the worst the farthest	

Comparatives in sentences				Notes
The computer is	cheaper noisier more expensive better	than	the photocopier.	Use the comparative to talk about two things.

Superlatives in sentences			Notes
This computer is	(one of) the cheapest (one of) the most popular	of all. in the store. this week.	Use the superlative to talk about groups of three or more things.

Questions with *which*		Answers
Which is bigger,	a house or a factory?	A factory is.
Which building is bigger,		A factory is bigger.

Adverbs of degree: *much, a lot, a little, a bit*					
A laptop	is	a little/a bit	more expensive	than	a tablet.
A used car		much/a lot	cheaper		a new car.

Adjectives with *too* and *not…enough*

Too + adjective			Notes
It's They're	too	small. noisy. expensive.	*too* = more than is good Use *too* + adjective.

Not…enough				Notes
It's They're	not	big quiet cheap	enough.	*enough* = the right amount It's not cheap enough. = It's too expensive.

Count and noncount nouns

Count nouns

Singular affirmative statements	
We have	a cookie.
There is	an egg.

Singular negative statements	
We don't have	a cookie.
There isn't	an egg.

Plural affirmative statements	
We have	two cookies.
There are	three eggs.

Plural negative statements	
We don't have	any cookies.
There aren't	any eggs.

Singular questions	
Do you have	a cookie?
	an egg?

Answers

Yes, we have a cookie.
No, we don't have an egg.

Plural questions		
Do you have	any	cookies?
		eggs?

Answers

Yes, we have some cookies.
No, we don't have any eggs.

Questions with *how many*		
How many	cookies eggs potatoes vegetables carrots	are there?

Answers	
There is	one cookie. one egg.
There are	many potatoes. a lot of vegetables. a few carrots.

Noncount nouns

Affirmative statements	
We have	some soup. two cans of soup.
There is	some soup.
There are	two cans of soup.

Negative statements	
We don't have	any soup. much soup.
There isn't	

Questions with *how much*		
How much	soup ice cream coffee spaghetti	is there?

Answers	
There is	one can of soup.
There are	two cartons of ice cream.
There is	a lot of coffee. a little spaghetti.

Direct and indirect objects

	Direct object	Indirect object	Notes
I'll give	the message	to him.	Some verbs, such as *give*, *send*, *show*, and *write*, can have two objects. When the indirect object follows the direct object, we use the prepositions *to* or *for*.
	Indirect object	**Direct object**	
I'll give	him	the message.	

OXFORD
UNIVERSITY PRESS

198 Madison Avenue
New York, NY 10016 USA

Great Clarendon Street, Oxford, OX2 6DP, United Kingdom

Oxford University Press is a department of the University of Oxford.
It furthers the University's objective of excellence in research, scholarship,
and education by publishing worldwide. Oxford is a registered trade
mark of Oxford University Press in the UK and in certain other countries

© Oxford University Press 2017

The moral rights of the author have been asserted

First published in 2017

2021 2020 2019

10 9 8 7 6

ISBN: 9 78 0 19 449377 2 STUDENT BOOK (PACK)

ISBN: 9 78 0 19 449302 4 STUDENT BOOK (PACK COMPONENT)

ISBN: 9 78 0 19 440479 2 OEVT APP

Printed in China

This book is printed on paper from certified and well-managed sources

ACKNOWLEDGMENTS

Back cover photograph: Oxford University Press building/David Fisher

Illustrations by: Cover, Jeff Mangiat / Mendola Artist Representatives. 5W
Infographics, p. 14, p. 19, p. 22, p. 31, p. 40, p. 56, p. 74, p. 87, p. 99, p. 104
(middle), p. 109 (right), p. 112, p. 122, p. 130, p. 136, p. 137, p. 161, p. 163
(bottom), p. 164, p. 169; Kenneth Batelmann p. 88, p. 117, p. 131; Annie
Bissett p. 135 (bus rules), p. 145; Dan Brown, p. 47, p. 103; Mark Collins p. 134;
Lyndall Culbertson p. 81, p. 92, p. 123 (realia), p. 147; Ken Dewar p. 89, p. 90
(food), p. 112 (first-aid kit), p. 155; Bill Dickson, p. 132, p. 146; Jody Emery p.
25, p. 26; Mike Gardner, p. 4, p. 6, p. 34, p. 58, p. 88, p. 104 (top), p. 114, p. 116,
p. 155, p. 162; Garth Glazier/AA Reps p. 115; John Goodwin, p. 8, p. 12, p. 26,
p. 109 (left), p. 149; Glenn Gustafson p. 128; Peter Hoey, p. 21, p. 23, p. 29, p.
85, p. 108, p. 113, p. 127, p. 157; Stewart Holmes/Illustration Ltd., p. 72; Mike
Hortens p. 36; Rod Hunt p. 33; Janos Jantner, p. 5, p. 20, p. 75; Ken Joudrey/
Munro Campagna p. 44; Uldis Klavins p. 19, p. 95; John Kurtz, p. 13, p. 17, p.
27, p. 55, p. 68, p. 111, p. 124, p. 130, p. 138; Jeffrey Lindberg p. 80; Deb Lofaso,
p. 10 (middle), p. 28, p. 37, p. 43, p. 70, p. 98, p. 123, p. 140, p. 163 (top), p.
168; Rose Lowry p. 140; Karen Minot p. 46 (realia), p. 60 (realia), p. 116, p. 162;
Peter Miserendino/P.T. Pie Illustrations p. 86; Jay Montgomery p. 11, p. 123
(people); Derek Mueller p. 4, p. 158, p. 160; Tom Newsom p. 46 (woman), p. 50;
Geo Parkin, p. 18, p. 76, p. 96, p. 97, p. 120, p. 152, p. 153, p. 159, p. 166; Terry
Paczko p. 32, p. 102; Karen Pritchett p. 106; Mark Riedy/Scott Hull Associates
p. 142; Aaron Sacco, p. xiii, p. 10 (top), p. 64, p. 110, p. 151; Martin Sanders, p.
38, p. 61; Jeff Sanson/Schumann & Co., p. 30; Jane Spencer p. 6, p. 34, p. 48, p.
62, p. 148; Reed Sprunger/Jae Wagoner Artists Rep., p. 170; Eric Velasquez p.
144; Brad Walker p. 156; Simon Williams/Illustration Ltd., p. 16, p. 100.

*We would also like to thank the following for permission to reproduce the following
photographs*: Click Bestsellers / Shutterstock.com, Cover; simonkr/Getty
Images, p. 2 (students); CZQS2000/STS/Getty Images, p. 3 (woman); asiseeit/
Getty Images, p. 14 (man studying); SnowWhiteimages/Shutterstock.com,
p. 14 (graduate); Hero Images/Getty Images, p. 14 (mechanic); ableimages/
Alamy Stock Photo, p. 22 (blonde woman); Blend Images/Alamy Stock Photo,
p. 22 (brunette woman); Hero Images Inc./Alamy Stock Photo, p. 28 (friends);
mimagephotography/Shutterstock.com, p. 40 (woman on phone); Blend
Images/Alamy Stock Photo, p. 40 (man on phone); racorn/Shutterstock.com,
p. 41 (co-workers); James Stuart Griffith/Shutterstock.com, p. 42 (for rent);
PeopleImages/Getty Images, p. 53 (car salesperson); Paul Matzner/Alamy
Stock Photo, p. 53 (mail carrier); Panther Media GmbH/Alamy Stock Photo, p.
53 (accountant); Ariel Skelley Blend Images/Newscom, p. 54 (businessmen);
Hill Street Studios/Getty Images, p. 60 (man paying bills); Alan Bozac/Alamy
Stock Photo, p. 65 (hard hat sign); DarkWeapon/Shutterstock.com, p. 65
(face mask sign); Wittybear/Shutterstock.com, p. 65 (eye wear sign); Alistair
Cotton/Alamy Stock Photo, p. 65 (safety gloves sign); fStop Images GmbH/
Alamy Stock Photo, p. 65 (apron sign); Ricky John Molloy/Getty Images, p.
66 (spilled watermelons); Westend61/Getty Images, p. 66 (tangled cords);
l i g h t p o e t/Shutterstock.com, p. 67 (copy machine); Image Source/Getty
Images, p. 67 (forklift); Fuse/Getty Images, p. 67 (mailing package); lsantilli/
Shutterstock.com, p. 67 (power tools); Shannon Fagan/Getty Images, p. 67
(typing letter); leungchopan/Shutterstock.com, p. 67 (businesswoman); Paula
Solloway/Alamy Stock Photo, p. 67 (office clerk); Andy Dean Photography/
Shutterstock.com, p. 67 (man); imtmphoto/Shutterstock.com, p. 69
(businessmen); michaeljung/Shutterstock.com, p. 69 (supermarket workers);
Juice Images/Alamy Stock Photo, p. 69 (factory workers); David Lees/Getty
Images, p. 70 (business people shaking hands); Panther Media GmbH/Alamy
Stock Photo, p. 73 (businesswoman); Jose Luis Pelaez Inc/Getty Images, p. 74
(paying bills); Lars Zahner/Alamy Stock Photo, p. 78 (woman jogging); Kzenon/
Shutterstock.com, p. 78 (man eating dinner); Jacob Lund/Shutterstock.com,
p. 82 (woman working); pink_cotton_candy/Getty Images, p. 82 (sick man);
Pressmaster/Shutterstock.com, p. 83 (office meeting); asiseeit/Getty Images,
p. 83 (restaurant manager); wavebreakmedia/Shutterstock.com, p. 84 (senior
volunteers); Bikeworldtravel/Shutterstock.com, p. 90 (woman); Blend Images/
Shutterstock.com, p. 92 (woman); EM Arts/Shutterstock.com, p. 95 (grapes);
Sheila Fitzgerald/Shutterstock.com, p. 95 (soup); Leonid Nyshko/Alamy
Stock Photo, p. 95 (yogurt); Lost Mountain Studio/Shutterstock.com, p. 95
(sausages); Tischenko Irina/Shutterstock.com, p. 98 (fruits & vegetables);
stevecoleimages/Getty Images, p. 102 (pharmacist); wavebreakmedia/
Shutterstock.com, p. 104 (x-ray); Lawrence Gibbens/Alamy Stock Photo, p. 107
(boy fallen off bike); Art Directors & TRIP/Alamy Stock Photo, p. 107 (woman
burned hand); Ljupco/Getty Images, p. 107 (stomachache); Andrey_Popov/
Shutterstock.com, p. 107 (sprained ankle); pcruciatti/Shutterstock.com, p.
118 (Apple store); Monkey Business Images/Shutterstock.com, p. 118 (man
on laptop); guruXOX/Shutterstock.com, p. 121 (woman using ATM); olaser/
Getty Images, p. 121 (man buying suit); Rawpixel.com/Shutterstock.com, p.
121 (online shopping); shooarts/Shutterstock.com, p. 123 (sweater); Evikka/
Shutterstock.com, p. 123 (socks); Mega Pixel/Shutterstock.com, p. 123 (tie);
MilanMarkovic/Getty Images, p. 125 (doctor's office receptionist); Alistair
Berg/Getty Images, p. 125 (hotel receptionist); Studio51/Alamy Stock Photo,
p. 126 (wallet); Tom Grundy/Alamy Stock Photo, p. 135 (no parking sign);
Michael Burrell/Alamy Stock Photo, p. 135 (no smoking sign); gmstockstudio/
Shutterstock.com, p. 135 (no left turn sign); jojoo64/Getty Images, p. 135 (no
right turn sign); Sergio Azenha/Alamy Stock Photo, p. 137 (brunette woman);
Klaus Tiedge/Getty Images, p. 137 (Hispanic man); mimagephotography/
Shutterstock.com, p. 137 (African-American man); PacoRomero/Getty Images,
p. 137 (Asian woman); Monty Rakusen/Getty Images, p. 139 (security guard);
Yongyuan Dai/Getty Images, p. 139 (bank teller); Creatas/Getty Images, p. 139
(airport security); Jim Young/Reuters, p. 140 (Sonia Sotomayor); Jeff Morgan
16/Alamy Stock Photo, p. 154 (flooding); Justin Lewis/Getty Images, p. 163
(zip-lining); Jose Luis Pelaez/Getty Images, p. 165 (man watching TV); Daniel
Allan/Getty Images, p. 165 (woman watching TV); davide piras/Alamy Stock
Photo, p. 165 (band concert); Greatstock/Alamy Stock Photo, p. 165 (coffee
shop); Juice Images Ltd/Getty Images, p. 167 (business conference); Jose Luis
Pelaez Inc/Getty Images, p. 167 (doctors); bikeriderlondon/Shutterstock.com,
p. 167 (engineers); Bo Zaunders/Getty Images, p. 168 (White House); lastdjedai/
Shutterstock.com, p. 168 (Niagara Falls); Alan Majchrowicz/Getty Images, p.
168 (Grand Canyon); dibrova/Shutterstock.com, p. 168 (San Francisco).